HOTSPOTS
THAILA

Written by Ryan Levitt, updated by Gary Hall
Original photography by Jacqueline Fryd

Published by Thomas Cook Publishing
A division of Thomas Cook Tour Operations Limited.
Company registration no. 3772199 England
The Thomas Cook Business Park, Unit 9, Coningsby Road,
Peterborough PE3 8SB, United Kingdom
Email: books@thomascook.com, Tel: + 44 (0) 1733 416477
www.thomascookpublishing.com

Produced by Cambridge Publishing Management Limited
Burr Elm Court, Main Street, Caldecote CB23 7NU

ISBN: 978-1-84848-100-8

First edition © 2007 Thomas Cook Publishing
This second edition © 2009
Text © Thomas Cook Publishing
Maps © Thomas Cook Publishing

Series Editor: Adam Royal
Production/DTP: Steven Collins

Printed and bound in Spain by GraphyCems

Cover photography: © Thomas Cook.

All rights reserved. No part of this publication may be reproduced, stored in
a retrieval system or transmitted, in any form or by any means, electronic,
mechanical, recording or otherwise, in any part of the world, without prior
permission of the publisher. Requests for permission should be made to the
publisher at the above address.

Although every care has been taken in compiling this publication, and the contents
are believed to be correct at the time of printing, Thomas Cook Tour Operations
Limited cannot accept any responsibility for errors or omissions, however caused,
or for changes in details given in the guidebook, or for the consequences of any
reliance on the information provided. Descriptions and assessments are based on
the author's views and experiences when writing and do not necessarily represent
those of Thomas Cook Tour Operations Limited.

CONTENTS

WHAT'S IN YOUR GUIDEBOOK?

Independent authors Impartial up-to-date information from our travel experts who meticulously source local knowledge.

Experience Thomas Cook's 165 years in the travel industry and guidebook publishing enriches every word with expertise you can trust.

Travel know-how Thomas Cook has thousands of staff working around the globe, all living and breathing travel.

Editors Travel-publishing professionals, pulling everything together to craft a perfect blend of words, pictures, maps and design.

You, the traveller We deliver a practical, no-nonsense approach to information, geared to how you really use it.

▶ *A golden Buddha at Wat Pho temple, Bangkok*

City
Large Town
Small Town
Motorway
Main Road
Minor Road
Airport

Thailand

Gulf of
Thailand

VIETNAM

PHNOM PENH

Ca Mau

Krong Preah
Sihanouk

Mu Koh Chang
National Park

Mekong

BURMA

Prachuap Khirikhan

Chumphon

Ranong

Koh Phangan
Koh Samui

Nakhon Si
Thammarat

Surat-Thani

Thung Song

Krabi

Pakmeng

Trang

Koh
Lanta

Hat Chao Mai
National Park

Mu Koh
Phi Phi

Phuket

Ao Phang-Nga
National Park

Hat Yai

Pattani

Narathiwat

MALAYSIA

Thailand

4

4

4

4

4

41

41

41

40I

44

42

43

N

Thailand

0   100 km

0   60 miles

Getting to know Thailand

They say that Thailand is the Land of Smiles – and what an apt saying it is. This beautiful nation located in Southeast Asia is one of the most popular tourist destinations in the world thanks to its enticing combination of friendly service, exotic culture and history, amazing cuisine and powder-soft beaches. For centuries, Westerners dreamed of getting their hands on this proud nation to add to their colonial treasures. While they never did (as locals are always proud to tell you), foreigners have swept into the country in an altogether different form – as tourists.

Thailand boasts a collection of resorts and destinations that other countries can only dream of. From the limestone cliffs and striking topography of the south to the laid-back, hippie islands in the Gulf of Thailand to the all-night parties on the mainland in the east – there's something to appeal to everyone. One visit certainly won't encapsulate everything there is to offer.

Western tourists have fallen for Thailand for many reasons. Not only is it an exceptionally easy country to travel around due to its extensive ferry, bus and air connections; it's also affordable. A euro or pound still goes far in these parts, making it easy for budget travellers to enjoy their holiday. Choosing a resort is probably the most difficult part of the trip. Those in search of wild nightlife and clubbing will adore the offerings of Bangkok and Pattaya. For rest and relaxation, choose Koh Samet and Krabi. Alternatively, Phuket offers a little of everything and is one of the most popular destinations as a result.

But Thailand isn't all about flying and flopping. It's a great place for experiential travellers looking to learn new skills, challenge their stamina, explore underwater worlds or learn about new cultures. Thousands of foreigners leave Thailand each year having taken cooking classes or studied with kickboxing masters. The country's reefs offer some of the best diving opportunities in the world – and PADI (Professional Association of Diving Instructors) certification here is reasonably priced. Why not combine your stay with a one-week course?

The tsunami of 2004 knocked the wind out of many communities, but these resorts are eager to welcome you whether it is your first visit or your hundredth. The Land of Smiles is back and bolder than ever.

🔺 *A colourful restaurant balcony in Hua Hin*

THE BEST OF THAILAND

To narrow down Thailand to ten 'bests' is almost an impossible task. Every day of your stay will bring you new memories and experiences that you will be sure can't be beat, but, if you're forced to choose, the following are not to be missed.

TOP 10 ATTRACTIONS

- **Explore the underwater world** with PADI-certified training at Phuket, Krabi, Trang, Koh Samet, Koh Phangan or Koh Phi Phi. If scuba seems too rigorous or time-consuming, throw on a mask and snorkel. It's easy and fun (see pages 51, 58, 64, 73, 76 and 82)!

- **A night in Pattaya's red-light district** You don't have to partake in its pleasures, but a night in Pattaya has to be seen to be believed. Prepare to goggle (see page 23).

- **A massage at sunset in Wat Pho** Hundreds of students come to learn ancient massage techniques at this Bangkok temple. Get the treatment of your life for next to nothing from one of the graduates who congregate near the school (see page 18).

- **Partying under the full moon on Koh Phangan** When the moon goes full, the hippies and backpackers come out to play. Head to the beach to live it up under a blanket of stars (see page 79).

- **Riding up the Chao Phraya River** Explore Bangkok from the river. Grab a long-tailed boat and away you go (see pages 14–15).

- **Horse riding on Hua Hin Beach** Ride down the coast at sunset and you will understand why the royal family makes this beach their second home (see page 37).

- **Buying Buddhas at Chatuchak** Thailand's biggest market offers many bargains. Come prepared with water and patience (see page 15).

- **Eating a yellow curry in Phuket** An outdoor patio. A sunset view. The sound of the sea. And a perfectly cooked seafood curry flavoured with turmeric (see pages 52–3). Ah bliss!

- **Cooking classes on Koh Samui** Head to the Radiance Restaurant at Spa Beach Resort to experience vegetarian cuisine at its finest – and then learn how to make it back home (see page 44).

- **Being James Bond in Ao Phang-Nga** Limestone cliffs plummet to powder beaches on James Bond Island, the location where Scaramanga's hideout was filmed in *The Man with the Golden Gun* (see page 80).

🔻 *A shrine under a Bodhi tree in Koh Phi Phi*

SYMBOLS KEY
The following symbols are used throughout this book:

ⓐ address ❶ telephone ❶ fax ⓦ website address ⓔ email
❶ opening times ❷ public transport connections ❶ important

The following symbols are used on the maps:

ℹ️ information office   ○ city
✉️ post office   ○ large town
🛍️ shopping   ○ small town
🛫 airport   ◼ POI (point of interest)
✚ hospital   ══ motorway
🚓 police station   ── main road
🚍 bus station   ── minor road
🚆 railway station   ── railway
✝️ cathedral
❶ numbers denote featured cafés, restaurants & evening venues

RESTAURANT RATINGS
The symbol after the name of each restaurant listed in this guide indicates the price of a three-course meal without drinks for one person:
£ under 180 baht   ££ 180–500 baht   £££ over 500 baht

❶ *Paradise found on Koh Phangan*

RESORTS
Places under the sun

Bangkok

The Thai capital, otherwise known as 'The Big Mango', is a vibrant, pulsating city that truly can say it's open all hours. Packed with historic sights, nightclubs, shopping districts and oh so much more, it is the gateway to Thailand, loved and loathed by all who visit.

Bangkok brings out strong emotions in visitors. Some say it is a black mark in Thai society with all the problems encountered by modern metropolises. Others admire its 'anything goes' mindset and revel in the pleasures offered by its canals and alleyways. Either way, it's a fascinating place to visit – whether for a day or an extended break.

Less than three centuries ago, Bangkok was a tiny fishing village on the Chao Phraya River, also known as the 'Mother River'. All that changed following the destruction of the former Thai capital in 1767 by the marauding Burmese. The royal family selected Bangkok as its new base, and the city sprung up around the Grand Palace.

⬤ *Long-tailed boats on the Chao Phraya River*

Bangkok has come a long way transportation-wise. Metered taxis are plentiful and a good choice, except during rush-hour gridlock. The highly modern BTS Skytrain and MRTA underground systems reach most destinations of interest, with the exception of areas near the river. For these, the Chao Phraya Express river boat is an excellent alternative, and great sightseeing in its own right. Connect from the Skytrain at Saphan Taksin.

Patpong is another must-do regardless of your views of red-light enticements. The night market is a great one-stop shop for souvenirs, while the bars, clubs and cabarets provide an eye-opening introduction to a different side of Thai culture, albeit one the Tourism Authority is less than happy to highlight.

THINGS TO SEE & DO

Chatuchak weekend market
Shop till you drop in this amazing market stacked with more than 8,000 stands specialising in everything from antiques to high fashion. The crowds can get overwhelming, so come prepared with lots of water and large stores of patience. Be prepared to hunt for the bargains. Sections are colour- and symbol-coded, so, if you are looking for something specific, check the maps dotted throughout the complex.
ⓐ Chatuchak Park, Thanon Phahon Yothin ⓛ 07.00–18.00 Sat & Sun
ⓝ BTS Skytrain stop: Mo Chit; MRTA subway stop: Chatuchak Park

Grand Palace
The original palace for the Thai royal family was constructed in 1782 when the capital was moved from Ayutthaya. Today, the palace is purely used for ceremonial events, but it remains an important symbol of power and religion. When visiting, be aware that there are strict dress codes that you must adhere to. Shorts, sandals and bare shoulders are strictly forbidden on both men and women.
ⓐ Thanon Na Phra Lan, Phra Nakhon ⓛ 08.30–15.30 ⓝ River boat stop: Tha Chang ⓘ Admission charge

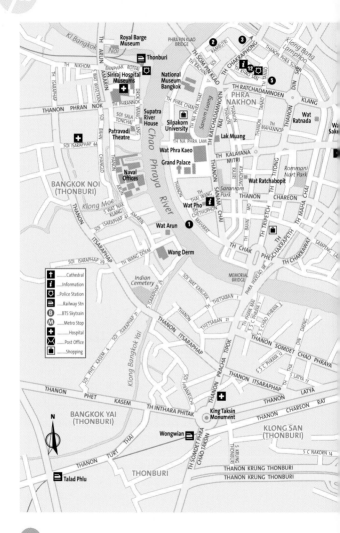

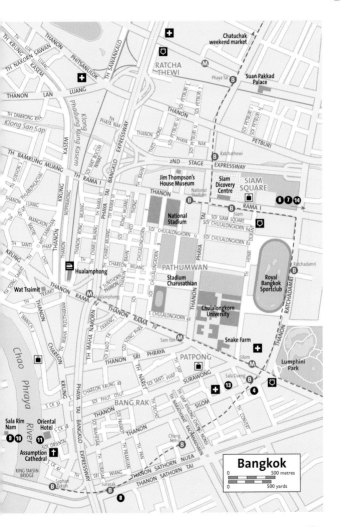

Jim Thompson's House Museum

Former CIA operative Jim Thompson single-handedly revived the Thai silk industry in the 1960s. See how he took his design sense and used it in his home at this spectacular re-creation of a traditional Thai teak house that combines local materials with international sensibilities.

ⓐ 6 Soi Kasemsan 2, Thanon Rama I ⓘ (0) 2216 7368
ⓦ www.jimthompsonhouse.com ⓛ 09.00–17.00 Ⓝ BTS Skytrain stop: National Stadium ❶ Admission charge

Khao San Road

Backpackers flock to this road, made famous by Alex Garland in his bestselling novel *The Beach*. Not as cheap as it used to be, but still worth a look.

ⓐ Thanon Khao San, Banglamphu Ⓝ River boat stop: Tha Phra Arthit

Lumphini Park

Take a breather by joining the masses in Bangkok's favourite public park. At dawn, this beloved green space buzzes with joggers looking for a bit of exercise before the day kicks into high gear.

ⓐ Thanon Rama IV, Pathum Wan ⓛ 04.30–21.00 Ⓝ BTS Skytrain stop: Sala Daeng; MRTA subway stop: Si Lom

National Museum Bangkok

This 'must-do' museum is the largest in Southeast Asia and boasts a collection of Thai art that is beyond compare.

ⓐ 4 Thanon Na Phrathat, Phra Nakhon, near National Theatre
ⓘ (0) 2224 1333 ⓦ www.thailandmuseum.com ⓛ 09.00–16.00 Wed–Sun
Ⓝ River boat stop: Tha Chang ❶ Admission charge

Wat Pho

This temple is the largest in Bangkok and boasts a massive gold-plated Buddha statue measuring over 46 m (151 ft) in length.

ⓐ Thanon Sanam Chai, Phra Nakhon ⓦ www.tourismthailand.org
ⓛ 08.00–17.00 Ⓝ River boat stop: Tha Tien ❶ Admission charge

The huge reclining Buddha at Wat Pho temple

Wat Saket and Golden Mount

Go to Wat Saket to climb Golden Mount, from which incredible views of the city can be enjoyed.

ⓐ 344 Thanon Chakraphatdiphong 🕐 07.30–17.30 ❶ Admission charge for Golden Mount only

TAKING A BREAK

Boh ££ ❶   Located right on the Chao Phraya River, this bohemian bar is popular with Bangkok's artsy types. ⓐ 230 Tha Tien, end of the pier
🕿 (0) 2622 3081 🕐 11.00–01.00 🅝 River boat stop: Tha Tien

Chabad House ££ ❷   Tuck into falafel and Middle Eastern yummies at this café that caters to Bangkok's massive visiting Israeli contingent.
ⓐ 96 Soi Rambutri, Banglamphu 🆆 www.chabadthailand.com
🕐 10.00–22.00 Sun–Thur, 10.00–15.00 Fri 🅝 River boat stop: Tha Phra Arthit

Kaloang Home Kitchen ££ ❸   Off the beaten track, but worth seeking out. Get a taxi and have them bring you to the very end of the street to enjoy simple seafood and Thai food in a relaxed riverside setting.
ⓐ 2 Thanon Sri Ayutthaya 🕐 11.00–22.00 🅝 River boat stop: Tha Thewet

The Bug & Bee ££ ❹   A clean, well-lit (and well air-conditioned) place to get a break from Silom's insanity. ⓐ 18 Thanon Silom
🆆 www.bugandbee.com 🕐 24 hours 🅝 BTS Skytrain stop: Sala Daeng; MRTA subway stop: Si Lom

AFTER DARK

Restaurants
May Kaidee ££ ❺   Bangkok's top vegetarian and vegan restaurant is this ever-popular eatery that boasts its own in-house cooking school.
ⓐ 59 Ratchadamnern, Banglamphu, behind Burger King
🆆 www.maykaidee.com 🕐 08.00–23.00

Vientiane Kitchen ££ ❻ Country-style Laotian cooking in a fun environment. Full stage show featuring Issaan (Northeastern Thai) band and dancers. ⓐ 8 Sukhumvit Soi 36, Klongtoey ❶ (0) 2258 6171 ⏰ 06.00–24.00 ⓝ BTS Skytrain stop: Thong Lo

Bed Supperclub £££ ❼ Sleep while you sup in this restaurant, where you are served in bed. Pyjamas, however, aren't the done thing. Instead, be prepared to dress up to the nines. Stay afterwards for the hip nightclub and bar. ⓐ 26 Sukhumvit Soi 11, Watthana ❶ (0) 2651 3537 ⓦ www.bedsupperclub.com ⏰ 19.30–01.00 ⓝ BTS Skytrain stop: Nana ❶ Call for reservations

Blue Elephant £££ ❽ The Thai food is good, but it's the cooking school that should grab your attention. Enjoy a lovely meal and then learn how to prepare it in your own kitchen! ⓐ 233 Thanon Sathorn Sai, Yannawa ❶ (0) 2673 9353 ⓦ www.blueelephant.com ⏰ 11.30–14.30, 18.30–22.00 ⓝ BTS Skytrain stop: Surasak

🔺 *The Khao San Road is always teeming with tourists*

Jester's £££ ❾ Fantastic international food in a 5-star restaurant with amazing views. ⓐ 1st Floor, Peninsula Hotel, 333 Thanon Charoen Nakorn, Klongsan ⓣ (0) 2861 2888 ⓦ www.bangkok.peninsula.com ⓝ BTS Skytrain stop: Saphan Taksin, followed by shuttle boat

Mei Jiang £££ ❿ Bangkok's top Chinese restaurant is this flagship eatery in the Peninsula Hotel. ⓐ 1st Floor, Peninsula Hotel, 333 Thanon Charoen Nakorn, Klongsan ⓣ (0) 2861 2888 ⓦ www.bangkok.peninsula. com ⓝ BTS Skytrain stop: Saphan Taksin, followed by shuttle boat

Le Normandie £££ ⓫ Top French cuisine in Bangkok's most famous (and expensive) eatery. Just what you'd expect from the Oriental Hotel's flagship restaurant. ⓐ 5th Floor, Oriental Hotel, 48 Oriental Ave, Surawongse ⓣ (0) 2236 0400 ⓦ www.mandarinoriental.com ⓛ 12.00–14.00, 19.00–22.30 ⓝ BTS Skytrain stop: Saphan Taksin; river boat stop: Oriental ⓘ Jacket and tie compulsory for men

Bars
Brick Bar ⓬ The Khao San Road shot into the land of boutique chic with the introduction of this design-focused combination hotel/bar. More expensive than other bars along the strip, it's also the coolest in terms of clientele. Live band nightly. ⓐ 265 Thanon Khao San, Banglamphu ⓣ (0) 2629 4477 ⓦ www.buddylodge.com ⓛ 14.00–24.00 ⓝ River boat stop: Tha Phra Arthit

DJ Station ⓭ This nightclub is a favourite with both the local and visiting gay community. Always packed, it's often hotter inside than out. ⓐ 8/6–8 Silom Soi 2, Silom ⓣ (0) 2266 4029 ⓦ www.dj-station.com ⓛ 22.00–02.00 ⓝ BTS Skytrain stop: Sala Daeng

Q Bar ⓮ Bangkok's hippest nightclub is this chic venue popular with Bangkok's moneyed set. ⓐ 34 Sukhumvit Soi 11, Watthana ⓣ (0) 2252 3274 ⓦ www.qbarbangkok.com ⓛ 20.00–01.00 ⓝ BTS Skytrain stop: Nana; MRTA subway stop: Sukhumvit

Pattaya

Pattaya isn't for everyone. Bold, glitzy, trashy and boasting a sleazy underbelly that gets splashed in the headlines on a regular basis, it's a beachfront resort town with many secrets. Originally a fishermen's village, it came into prominence during the Vietnam War when American GIs on rest and recuperation leave flocked to the region to live it up during their breaks from the battles raging two nations over. Girls, booze and anything else money could buy followed in their wake, and Pattaya's reputation was established.

While Pattaya still has a carnal flavour, it is trying to clean up its act. Whether this is due to a new-found morality or global pressure remains to be seen. Americans are no longer the driving force behind the freewheeling attitudes, having been replaced by Brits, Germans, Russians and moneyed residents of other Asian nations such as Japan and Korea. Their misdeeds are often reported in the Thai media as criminal influences from all these countries infiltrating the drug and prostitution rings of the city.

If all this makes Pattaya sound like some sort of devilish playground, fear not. There are still lots of attractions, beaches and sights worthy of exploration and enjoyment. Thai middle-class families from Bangkok often make the trip down to the city, drawn by the convenient access from the capital, affordable resorts, wealth of golf courses and extensive diversions. If you're looking for the authentic Thai experience, however, then this is not the resort for you. The city's close ties with America have transformed it into a pocket of the superpower complete with branches of Pizza Hut, McDonald's and every other fast-food chain you can think of.

Instead, scratch under the surface to see what drew visitors to Pattaya in the first place. Avoid the girly bars and cluttered main beach and you'll find a city of friendly locals eager to show off Thailand's first resort town.

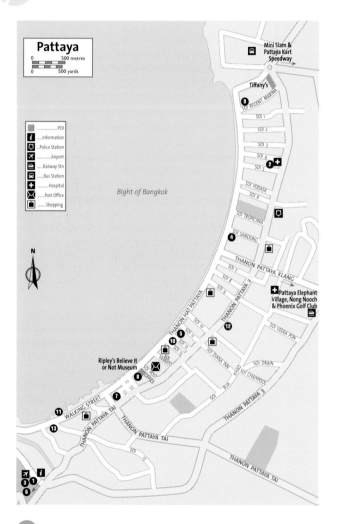

Pattaya

0	500 metres
0	500 yards

POI
i ....Information
....Police Station
✈ ....Airport
....Railway Stn
🚌 ....Bus Station
➕ ....Hospital
✉ ....Post Office
🛍 ....Shopping

Bight of Bangkok

N

Mini Siam &
Pattaya Kart
Speedway

Tiffany's

SOI REGENT MARINA
SOI 1
SOI 2
SOI 3
SOI 4
SOI 5
SOI YODASK
SOI 6
SOI TROPICANA
SOI SAIROONG
THANON PATTAYA KLANG
SOI 7
SOI 8
SOI 9
SOI 10
THANON HAI PATTAYA
THANON PATTAYA
SOI DIANA INN
SOI DRAIN
SOI VEERA PON
SOI CHAIYPOOL
THANON PATTAYA 3
WALKING STREET
THANON PATTAYA TAI
SOI 11
THANON PATTAYA TAI

Pattaya Elephant
Village, Nong Nooch
& Phoenix Golf Club

Ripley's Believe It
or Not Museum

BEACHES

Due to rapid development and a lack of effective waste management and treatment centres, Pattaya Beach is not recommended for swimming. On seriously hot days, the coliform count soars, making it a bad idea to even contemplate dipping your toes in the sea unless you want to face serious health challenges later on.

The Thai government is making great efforts to combat problems, but success has been limited. In 1992, Pattaya was granted funds for the construction of a water treatment centre – the first resort in the country to be given such a facility. Even with this addition, however, South Pattaya Beach remains pretty much off-limits to all but the most foolhardy swimmers. If in doubt, do as most visitors do and stick to the swimming pools and amenities of your chosen resort hotel.

⬥ *A view over Pattaya*

As Pattaya lacks good beach facilities and has a somewhat sleazy reputation, you might be asking yourself why anyone would choose to visit. The answer is affordability. Five-star properties are available at good prices, and the quality of service you receive once you check in is comparable to top hotels around the world. Pattaya Beach experiences a repeat visitor rate of approximately 50 per cent, although most of that number hails from other parts of Thailand or nearby Asian nations.

Further south is the more family-friendly option of Jomtien, which due to its location around a bend from Pattaya Bay is much quieter than its more raucous neighbour. Resorts tend to be much smaller in scale and cater to Thai travellers who favour sporting facilities, authentic Thai food and a more carefree vibe. Jomtien is also the beach of choice for Pattaya's large number of gay visitors. Relax in the sun on a deckchair with an umbrella, hired for a few baht from the various stallholders who line the sand.

THINGS TO SEE & DO

Mini Siam

Feel like a giant at this Lilliput-sized land that shows off Thailand's greatest landmarks in miniature. Popular with kids and kids at heart.
ⓐ 387 Moo, 6 Thanon Sukhumvit ⓣ (0) 3872 7333 ⓛ 07.00–20.00
❶ Admission charge

Nong Nooch Tropical Garden

Located a short 18-km (11-mile) hop out of the city, this great tourist attraction is one of the best in Pattaya. Showcasing a concentrated dose of everything great about Thailand, Nong Nooch offers Thai dancing performances, elephant rides, Thai boxing matches, music and introductions to Thai cultural traditions. Shuttles depart from all major Pattaya and Jomtien properties at 08.30 or 13.15 every day. Return trips can also be arranged. Call the park in advance to book a space.
ⓐ Reach via Thanon Sukhumvit, Sattahip ⓣ (0) 3842 9321
ⓦ www.nongnoochtropicalgarden.com ❶ Admission charge

⬤ Monks walking along the beach at Pattaya

Pattaya Elephant Village

Children love the elephants and animal acts at this village. Daily shows start at 14.30. Half-hour jungle treks on elephant back are also available.

ⓐ Reach via Siam Country Club Road east from Thanon Sukhumvit
ⓣ (0) 3824 9818 ⓦ www.elephant-village-pattaya.com
ⓘ Admission charge

Pattaya Kart Speedway

A 1-km (²/₃-mile) loop track that's a blast for anyone, young or old, who loves life in the fast lane. Priced according to the class of kart you choose. Suitable for kids aged 8 and up.

ⓐ Thanon Thep Prasit Soi 9, Jomtien ⓣ (0) 3842 2044 ⓛ 09.00–16.00
ⓘ Admission charge

Phoenix Golf Club

There are many championship golf courses in the Pattaya area; this is one of the better ones. Bangkok's middle classes flock here to enjoy a round or two. Weekends are especially busy.

ⓐ 4 km (2½ miles) off Thanon Sukhumvit at Kilometer 158 ⓣ (0) 3823 9391 ⓛ 06.00–16.00 ⓘ Admission charge

Ripley's Believe It or Not Museum

It isn't all that pretty, but this tacky collection of global oddities is sure to shock you and put a smile on your face. There's nothing educational about the place. Instead, it's a bit like going to a circus specialising in freaks and weirdos.

ⓐ 3rd Floor, Royal Garden Plaza, 218 Thanon Hat Pattaya ⓣ (0) 3871 0294
ⓦ www.ripleysthailand.com ⓛ 10.00–23.00 ⓘ Admission charge

Tiffany's

Pattaya's most glamorous women are actually men – and you can find them performing every night at Tiffany's. The theatre itself looks something like a wedding cake laced with neon icing. While a transvestite lip-synch musical may not be top of your list of attractions, you'll change your mind rapidly after you see the glorious concoctions on stage. One of the biggest events of the year is the annual Miss Tiffany's contest, which is battled out on national television.

🅐 464 Thanon Pattaya 2 🅣 (0) 3842 1700 🅦 www.tiffany-show.co.th
🅛 Multiple performances every night 🅘 Admission charge

TAKING A BREAK

Moonshine Place ££ ❶ If you're staying around Jomtien, then this eatery is worth calling in at – especially if you like your dishes well spiced. Choose from the great Thai or less successful Mexican meals on the menu. If you want to eat on the beach or back in your room,

🔺 *The 'girls' performing at Tiffany's*

takeaway is offered. ⓐ Thanon Hat Jomtien at Soi 6, Jomtien ⓣ (0) 3823 1956 ⓛ 07.00–02.00

PIC Kitchen ££ ❷   This collection of air-conditioned and open-air teak pavilions is a great place for a casual lunch on a hot day. Let fragrant breezes cool you as you tuck into some of Pattaya's finest and freshest seafood dishes. As an added plus, a live band plays every evening from 19.00. ⓐ Pattaya 2 Soi 5 ⓣ (0) 3842 8374 ⓦ www.pic-kitchen.com ⓛ 11.00–14.00, 18.00–24.00

Vientiane ££ ❸   Thai and Lao dishes served up at a large and comfortable eatery. The menu is extensive. Solve language issues by pointing at the number of the item you want. ⓐ 485/10, Moo 10, Thanon Pattaya Tai 2 ⓣ (0) 3842 2673 ⓛ 10.30–23.30

AFTER DARK

Restaurants
Lobster Pot ££ ❹   It may not offer the best seafood in town, but it's certainly the showiest. Water tanks and a massive dining area bring in both locals and foreigners to its lively tables. ⓐ 228 Thanon Hat Pattaya ⓣ (0) 3842 6083 ⓛ 12.00–01.00

Shere E Punjab ££ ❺   Authentic northern Indian cuisine in an intimate setting. Pull up a chair at one of the candlelit outdoor tables or enjoy air-conditioned comfort inside the main restaurant. ⓐ 216 Soi 11, Thanon Hat Pattaya ⓣ (0) 3842 0158 ⓛ 12.30–23.00

Steak Bao ££ ❻   Popular with the testosterone-fuelled, this sports bar is packed almost every hour of the day. The steak served up is better than average. Makes for a friendly and fun place when you need a filling meal. ⓐ Thanon Theppaya at Soi 12, Jomtien ⓣ (0) 3842 0492 ⓛ 24 hours

Alt Heidelberg £££ ❼ Built to accommodate Pattaya's vast German visitor market, this pricey restaurant dishes up good-quality German specialities including fresh handmade sausages, sauerkraut and German beer on tap. ⓐ 273 Thanon Hat Pattaya ⓣ (0) 3842 1258 ⓛ 09.00–01.00

Benihana £££ ❽ Sure, it's an American-Japanese chain with a cheesy theme, but it's a great place to come if you want a laugh and can't stand the idea of another green curry. ⓐ 2nd level, Royal Garden Plaza, 218 Thanon Hat Pattaya ⓣ (0) 3841 2120 ⓛ 11.00–22.00

Henry J Bean's £££ ❾ The large military and American expat presence has brought with it almost every fast-food chain imaginable. This Tex-Mex eatery is one of the better ones. ⓐ Amari Orchid Resort, Thanon Hat Pattaya ⓣ (0) 3842 8161 ⓛ 11.00–01.00

Bars

Hopf Brewery ❿ An in-house jazz band and on-site microbrewery make this watering hole a cut above the rest. ⓐ 219 Thanon Hat Pattaya ⓣ (0) 3871 0650 ⓛ 05.00–late

Lucifer ⓫ This club wouldn't feel out of place in some of the more ritzy districts of Bangkok. Lined with velvet furnishings and plenty of gilt, it's the venue of choice for visitors from the capital looking to club in posh surroundings. ⓐ Walking Street ⓣ (0) 3871 0216 ⓛ 22.00–02.30

Shenanigans ⓬ Generally considered to be the best expat bar in the city, it offers genuine Irish beer and a welcoming, friendly atmosphere. ⓐ 'The Avenue' Shopping Center, Thanon Pattaya 2 ⓣ (0) 3842 8161 ⓦ www.shenanigans-pattaya.com ⓛ 10.00–late

Tony's ⓭ Of all the clubs in Pattaya, this is probably the best. Less crowded with bar girls than most other establishments, it boasts a good sound system, pool tables and lots of theme evenings. ⓐ 139/15 Walking Street ⓣ (0) 3842 5795 ⓦ www.tonydisco.com ⓛ 20.30–late

Koh Chang

Koh Chang is the largest island in a collection of about 50 located off the southeastern mainland coast of Thailand close to the Cambodian border. The island serves as the base for a national marine park, and many come for the express purpose of exploring the archipelago. Koh Chang developed more recently than Thailand's other major resort communities, and much of the rainforest and mangrove forests for which the island is renowned remains untouched, as over 95 per cent of the land area is protected national park. If you're looking for a combination of 5-star luxury with pristine wilderness, then look no further.

BEACHES

Most of the island's beaches and the great bulk of its resorts are located on the west coast. Hat Sai Khao, aka White Sand Beach, is the epicentre of tourist business on Koh Chang, and the place most people go when they first get off the ferry. Many travellers are drawn by the nightlife and services along the northern stretch of the main road. Towards the southern end are low-cost guesthouses and a growing coterie of middle- and upper-scale establishments.

High-end travellers tend to gravitate to the area 4 km (2½ miles) south at Khlong Phrao, where there are rentable bungalows and boutique resort properties. Hat Kaibae, at the southern end of Khlong Phrao Bay, is rapidly gentrifying, and no longer fits the description of a backpacker haven. Further south, Lonely Beach (Hat Tha Nam) also doesn't quite fit its old nickname, but is still relatively quiet and youth-culture oriented. At the far southern end, Bang Bao has a charming village of guesthouses, restaurants and dive shops built out onto the bay along a 1-km (²⁄₃-mile) fishing pier.

In the other direction, the southeastern tip features a cluster of resorts and businesses that traditionally served Thai family holidaymakers. Increasingly, new businesses are targeting Western visitors who want a quieter and more traditional island experience.

◆ *Go on an elephant trek in Koh Chang*

THINGS TO SEE & DO

Diving & snorkelling
The south coast of Koh Chang and the reefs surrounding nearby islands offer some of the best diving experiences in Thailand. It's less crowded than other centres, so you won't find the tourist hordes or coral bleaching problems that other locales have. Diving operators can be found all along the west coast.

Elephant treks
Explore the forested interior on elephant back for an experience you will never forget. Alternatively, visit some retired members of the elephant community as they live out their golden years in their natural habitat at the Ban Kwan Elephant Camp. Visits involve opportunities to feed, bathe and ride the gentle animals.
ⓐ 2 km (1¹⁄₃ miles) inland from Ban Khlong Son ⓣ (0) 1919 3995
ⓛ 08.30–17.00

Khlong Phu Falls
While they aren't as revered as the Than Ma Yom Waterfall (*see below*), these falls located at Ao Khlong Phrao are much more accessible. It is an easy ten-minute journey by taxi or motorbike from Hat Sai Khao.
ⓘ National Park admission charge

Than Ma Yom Waterfall
Located on the east side of the island, this waterfall (actually a collection of three waterfalls) is reached following a one-hour, 4-km (2¹⁄₂-mile) hike along a well-marked trail from either Ban Dan Mai or Tha Than Ma Yom.
ⓘ National Park admission charge

TAKING A BREAK

Ban Nuna Restaurant & Café £ The best light-bites option on Koh Chang, Ban Nuna offers Thai, Western and sandwich choices to the hungry masses. ⓐ Hat Sai Khao ⓣ (0) 8 1821 4202 ⓛ 07.00–22.00

Funky Hut Resort ££ Despite the name, this is a family resort whose food enjoys an excellent reputation. ⓐ 2 km (1⅓ miles) south of Tha Dan Kao ferry pier ⓣ (0) 3958 6177 ⓦ www.funkyhut-thailand.com ⓛ 08.00–21.00

Tonsai ££ An 'old-school' Koh Chang establishment, furnished with scatter cushions, hammocks and low wooden tables. Sit cross-legged or lounge on the seats as you tuck into Thai-style treats lovingly prepared by the friendly kitchen staff. ⓐ North end of Hat Sai Kao ⓣ (0) 8 9895 7229 ⓛ 11.00–22.00

AFTER DARK

Restaurants
Oodie's Place £ The guitar-playing owner is proud of his 20 years as a 'wetback' on Chicago's South Side, soaking up the blues. Now every night he puts his experience to good use with his own band and any visiting musicians who want to jam. ⓐ North side of Hat Sai Kao ⓣ (0) 8 1853 1271 ⓛ 12.00–late

The Bay Restaurant & Bar ££ An unprepossessing place on Bang Bao's fishing village pier. The catch comes straight from the boat and on to your plate. ⓐ Bang Bao pier ⓣ (0) 8 1773 4680 ⓛ 12.00–22.30

Thor's Royal Thai Cuisine ££ The *Guardian*'s Emily Barr called it the best meal of her life. Maybe you can't remember your whole life, but really very, very good Thai and European food. ⓐ Hat Sai Khao, at Koh Chang Hut Resort ⓣ (0) 3055 1160 ⓛ 08.00–late

Invito £££ Thailand meets Italy in a new hillside garden villa location, serving up Italian cuisine that wouldn't be out of place in Rome. The wood-fired pizzas are especially tasty. ⓐ Hat Sai Khao, south side ⓣ (0) 3955 1460 ⓛ 16.00–late

Hua Hin & Cha Am

Before there were any other Thai resort towns, there were Hua Hin and Cha Am. Developed in the 1920s to accommodate Bangkok's élite, these two neighbouring fishing villages were some of the first beachside communities to be linked by rail with the capital, and they experienced a boom in interest as a result. The Thai royal family immediately created a craze for the region after they chose the seaside towns as their favoured holiday destination. They remain firm fans, frequently decamping to their palace located just to the north of Hua Hin.

The peaceful, serene vibe owes much to the popularity of Pattaya during the 1960s. Pattaya lured many of the towns' tourists away due to its cheap rates and eye-opening nightlife. Hua Hin and Cha Am chose to remain as sleepy as they ever were and experienced a temporary downturn as a result. Luckily, many are rediscovering their joys and the tourists are coming back in bigger numbers.

BEACHES

Due to a rediscovery of Hua Hin by residents of the capital, there are many building works going on along the beachfront. Many of these developments are new resort properties catering to foreign and domestic tourists. As a result, some stretches of the beach look uncared for and litter is an issue. Hua Hin is also battling a major problem with sewage treatment, just as Pattaya did during the early 1990s.

For a more authentic beach experience, go north to the sister town of Cha Am. While it lacks most of the facilities enjoyed by Thailand's other major resort communities and much of Hua Hin's casual charm, its beach is cleaner than that of its next-door neighbour. Most of Cha Am is used by Thai travellers, with foreigners selecting the resorts – and therefore the beaches – of Hua Hin. As such, you'll find Cha Am's beaches relatively empty during the week, when most visitors are stuck in their office buildings in Bangkok.

THINGS TO SEE & DO

Horse riding

Soak in the sun from the back of a pony on Hua Hin's stretch of sand. Choose to have either a guided ride led by a walking groom or a leisurely ride with a mounted guide. Numerous operators offer the opportunity, so be sure to shop around to get the best rates. Expect to pay about 600 baht an hour. You'll find sellers at various locations along the beach.

Marukhathaiyawan Palace

Formerly the summer palace for the Thai royal family, this beautiful retreat is now open to the public.

ⓐ Rama VI Camp, Petchkasem Road between Hua Hin and Cha Am
ⓛ 08.30–16.00 weekdays, 08.30–17.00 weekends ⓘ Admission charge

ⓞ Beach activities at Cha Am

⬥ *The path to the sea at Hua Hin*

Night market

Pick up cheap souvenirs, tasty treats and soak in the after-dark buzz. If the offerings don't impress, then check out the late-opening shops that congregate around Hua Hin's central seafront.

ⓐ Thanon Dechanuchit, Hua Hin, between Petchkasem Road and the railway tracks ⓛ Dusk–late

Phetchaburi

Located about an hour away from Hua Hin and Cha Am, this ancient town makes an excellent day excursion. Many kings used the city as a second residence for selected sons as a place to groom the heir to the throne. The hilltop summer palace is the highlight of any visit, but numerous *wats* (temples) and artefacts also draw the crowds.

ⓐ Petchkasem Road/Hwy 4, about 70 km (42 miles) north of Cha Am

TAKING A BREAK

World News Coffee £ Drinks, light snacks and internet plus air-con, comfortable seating and English-language newspapers. ⓐ 33 Thanon Naresdamri (next to Hilton Hotel), Hua Hin ⓣ (0) 3253 8999 ⓦ www.worldnewscoffee.com ⓛ 08.00–22.30

Kaenchan Beach Hotel ££ The restaurant in this pleasant 3-star hotel is well known for providing feasts for visiting tour groups. Beachside seating is also available. ⓐ 241/4 Thanon Ruamjit, Cha Am ⓣ (0) 3247 0777 ⓛ 07.00–22.00

Ye Olde Buffalo Tavern ££ This British-owned restaurant serves steaks of all shapes and sizes. Many UK travellers come just for the traditional fry-up breakfast. ⓐ 8 Thanon Naresdamri, Hua Hin ⓣ (0) 3253 0087 ⓦ www.buffalobillshuahin.com ⓛ 08.30–02.30

AFTER DARK

Restaurants

Chao Lay ££ There are a number of restaurants on Hua Hin's wharf, and Chao Lay is acknowledged to be one of the best. Select your fish meal from the tanks of live ones out front before you sit down. ⓐ 15 Thanon Naresdamri, Hua Hin ① (0) 3251 3436 ① 10.00–22.00

Da Vinci's ££ With chic décor and a delicious menu, this boutique eatery offers great food in a designer setting. European dishes are the speciality, making it a good option when you get tired of Thai food. ⓐ 274/5 Thanon Ruamjit, Cha Am ① (0) 3247 1871 ① 09.00–22.30 (high season)

Itsara ££ This Thai restaurant dates back to when Hua Hin became a major pleasure destination in the 1920s. Located next to the beach, it offers delicious dishes in a relaxed, atmospheric setting. ⓐ 7 Thanon Napkehard, Hua Hin ① (0) 3253 0574 ⓦ www.itsara-huahin.com ① 10.00–22.00

Meekaruna Seafood ££ While the seafood menu is great and well selected, it's the fresh catch of the day that should draw you. Options change daily. ⓐ 26/1 Thanon Naresdamri, Hua Hin ① (0) 3251 1932 ① 16.00–22.00

Bars

O'Neil's Irish Pub Favoured expat drinking den due to its Irish pub stylings. ⓐ 5 Thanon Poonsuk, Hua Hin ① (0) 3251 1932 ① 12.15–01.00

Koh Samui

In search of the perfect Thai beach, the hippies of the 1970s arrived on the island of Koh Samui and thought they had found paradise. Less populated or developed than any other beachside pocket of the country, the island soon began to accommodate these travellers in search of the 'real' Thailand with beach huts and hostels hastily constructed to meet demand.

Located 84 km (52 miles) off the east coast in the Gulf of Thailand, Koh Samui is today a shadow of its once pristine self, boasting just as many American fast-food joints as its mainland counterparts. You can still see pockets of what drew early travellers to its Eden-like wilderness the further inland or southwest you go away from the main airport and ferry terminals.

Hotel development, while booming, isn't as unregulated as in other locales such as Pattaya or Phuket. Recent additions have brought a boutique feel to this island in the form of small-scale, chic resorts designed by local architects.

BEACHES

The busiest beach of the lot is Chaweng, located on the east coast just south of the island's international airport. Here is where you will find the bulk of Koh Samui's resort-style and package-tourist properties in addition to the businesses that thrive on this kind of traveller to make ends meet – think fast-food outlets, cut-price tailors and extremely loud discos.

Further south is Lamai, a once beautiful bay that now suffers from development problems in the form of untreated sewage. Both Chaweng and Lamai are popular with British holidaymakers.

The north-coast beaches are popular with Europeans such as Swedes, Germans and Norwegians due to their quieter nightlife and smaller-scale accommodation options. Beaches on this shore include Big Buddha, Bo Phut and Mae Nam.

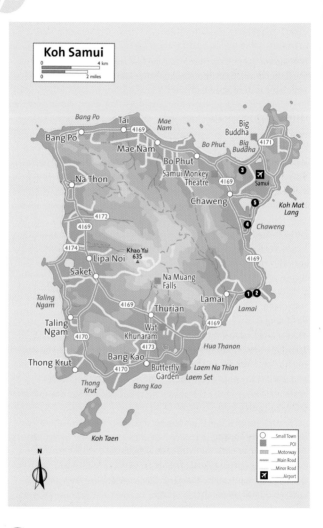

For secluded coves offering less sand but more secrecy, head to the southwest corner of the island. Here, you won't find many large-scale developments, but instead private residences and intimate hotels. You won't find the same standard of facilities or comfort, but you will get a bit more authenticity for your baht.

THINGS TO SEE & DO

Big Buddha
This 24-m (79-ft) tall Buddha is a well-known landmark on Koh Samui. Historically, however, it holds little importance. Connected to the main island by a causeway, it's open all day and makes for a pleasant diversion.
ⓐ Ko Faan

Butterfly Garden
A peaceful park that visitors can wander through. Admire the myriad butterflies during your gentle stroll.
ⓐ Southeast corner of 4170 Road near Laen Din ☏ (0) 7742 4020
🕙 09.00–17.00 ❶ Admission charge

Na Muang Falls
Popular with visitors as part of an all-island tour package, these waterfalls are most stunning at the end of the rainy season in December when water levels surge. The falls themselves are a 5-km (3-mile) walk from the road. If you can't cope with the heat, pre-book an elephant trek upon arrival.
ⓐ Off Route 4169 across from Wat Khunaram

Samui Monkey Theatre
Watch trained monkeys show off their skills at this comic show that features dozens of our primate friends in a variety of situations. Kids love it.
ⓐ 4169 Road, south of Bo Phut ☏ (0) 7724 5140 🕙 Show times: 10.30, 14.00, 16.00 daily ❶ Admission charge

Wat Khunaram

Backpackers and hippies flock here for a blessing with water from the resident monk. Just don't be put off by the temple's mummified founder whose remains can be seen sitting encased in glass in a small building behind the temple.

ⓐ 4169 Road, southwest of Lamai

TAKING A BREAK

Buddy Beer & Shark Bar ££ ❶ You can get a good meal at the adjoining Chom Lay Restaurant, but it's the beer that keeps the punters coming to this Samui branch of the Khaosan icon. ⓐ 173/24 Robkoh Road, Lamai Beach ⓣ (0) 7745 8080 ⓛ 11.00–02.00

Radiance Restaurant at Spa Beach Resort £££ ❷ People come from around the world to experience the award-winning vegetarian specialities and famous detox treatments at this Thai eatery located right on the beach. The cooking school is well worth checking out if you want to discover what wonders you can perform with local vegetables. ⓐ Lamai Beach ⓣ (0) 7723 0855 ⓦ www.thesparesorts.net ⓛ 07.00–21.30

AFTER DARK

Restaurants
The Mangrove £££ ❸ This delightfully located and designed restaurant is considered by many to be the best on Koh Samui. While its location near Bo Phut on the road between Bo Phut and Big Buddha, away from the main tourist traps, makes it inconvenient to get to, it is definitely worth the trip. Dining is open-air near a forest of mangroves. The international dishes are presented beautifully. ⓐ Airport Road, Big Buddha Beach ⓣ (0) 7742 7584 ⓛ 17.00–late

Poppies £££ ❹ The perfect place for a spot of romance, Poppies offers great seafood in a thatch pavilion with beach views. The menu changes frequently. Live jazz music adds a pleasant touch. ⓐ South end of Chaweng Beach ⓣ (0) 7742 2419 ⓦ www.poppiessamui.com ⓛ 06.30–24.00

Zico's Brazilian Grill & Bar £££ ❺   Feel like you're in Brazil at this meat-friendly eatery that serves up skewers of well-cooked delicacies spiced South American style. Brazilian performers and music add to the Rio-lite flavour. ⓐ Centara Grand Resort, Chaweng ⓣ (0) 7723 1560 ⓦ www.zicossamui.com ⓛ 19.00–22.30

⬤ *Beach huts on Koh Samui's eastern coast*

Phuket

In 2004, most of the west coast of the island of Phuket was devastated by the Boxing Day tsunami. Many of the images of Thailand under siege were filmed here as visitors and locals battled for survival in the aftermath. Today, these resorts are brighter and better than ever before. Developers used the tragedy as an excuse to undertake much-needed repairs and renovations, and capacity now exeeds pre-tsunami levels.

It may sound in poor taste to look at the tsunami in such positive terms, but many of Phuket's residents depend on the tourism industry for survival. Refreshed and revamped resorts bring employment back to a community that went through so much just a few short years ago. Tourists are more valued than ever before.

Like Pattaya, Phuket has gone through an explosive period of mass development over the past few decades, transforming itself from an

⬥ *Traders in a Phuket street*

island of small fishing communities to one of Thailand's most popular resort destinations. Much of Phuket's traffic comes from the moneyed classes of other Asian nations such as Singapore and Hong Kong. This is due to the variety of facilities and resort levels available.

Families especially love the properties of Phuket, as most resorts feature full-scale facilities at sensible prices. If you do decide to bring the tots, you might want to avoid the trappings of Kata/Karon and Patong unless you want to hear your little one ask you what 'fully nude review' means.

While the beaches of Phuket are pleasant enough, it's the lush interior that makes the destination such a complete package. Don't limit yourself to the golden sands. Instead, try renting a car to explore the hills and jungles that drew the first travellers oh so many years ago.

BEACHES

Whether you like your beach busy and pulsing with activity or secluded and private, you're bound to find what you're looking for on Phuket. The busiest of the lot is Patong Beach, a heaving mass of humanity that calls itself home to everything from 5-star luxury resorts to no-star temporary love hotels. You'll have to put up with a lot of hassle from touts, but, if you're looking for loads of watersports and activities, then you've come to the right place.

North of Patong are Kamala Bay, Pan Sea Beach and Surin Beach – perfect for those who want a bit more privacy yet still want to be within a stone's throw of Patong's trappings.

Further north still is Bang Tao Beach, headquarters of the Laguna Resort Complex. This area hosts five large-scale luxury resorts that work together in partnership to control one of Phuket's most beautiful seaside areas. While the beach is stunning, it is a bit out of the way if you are looking for nightlife; Patong is just that bit too far to warrant a day trip.

At the far north are the beaches of Sirinath National Park – true paradise for nature lovers. This is the place to head for if you want a Robinson Crusoe experience; just don't expect anything in the way of

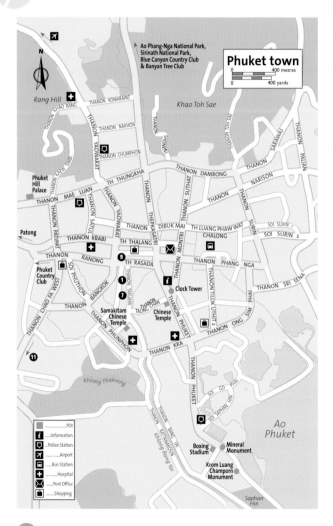

Phuket town

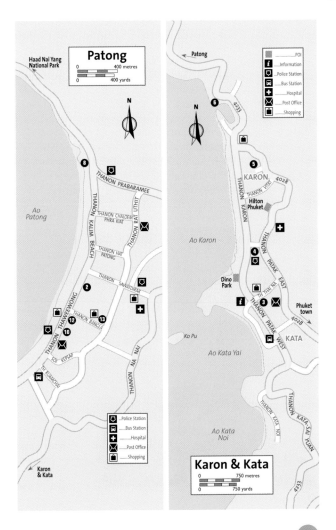

Patong

0   400 metres
0   400 yards

Haad Nai Yang National Park

Ao Patong

THANON PRABARAMEE
THANON KALIM BEACH
THANON CHALOEM PHRA KIAT
THANON RAT UTHIT
THANON HAT PATONG
THANON SAWATDIRAK
THANON THANEEVWONG
THANON BANGLA
THANON NA NAI
SOI KEPSAP
TH RUMJCHAI

Karon & Kata

...Police Station
...Bus Station
...Hospital
...Post Office
...Shopping

Patong

...POI
i **...Information**
...Police Station
...Bus Station
...Hospital
...Post Office
...Shopping

KARON
4028
THANON UTHIT
THANON KARON
Hilton Phuket
THANON PATAK EAST
Ao Karon
Dino Park
TH THAI NA
THANON PATAK WEST
Phuket town
4028
KATA
Ko Pu
Ao Kata Yai
THANON KATA NOI
THANON KATA SAI YUAN
Ao Kata Noi

Karon & Kata

0   750 metres
0   750 yards

luxuries or amenities. Bring a sleeping bag and feel like you're in heaven under the stars. Snorkellers and divers will especially adore the massive coral reef located just 1.4 km (³⁄₄ mile) offshore in shallow waters.

The most northern beach of all is Mai Khao, home to the JW Marriott resort and annual giant sea turtle hatchings.

Back down south, past Patong, you will find Kata, Kata Noi and Karon beaches. Here is where you will get the best bargains on the island. Resorts and beaches are developed but not to the point of chaos, although this is changing rapidly as interest in the area increases. Go now before it loses its character and great stretches of long sand.

Further south are Rawai, Chalong and Nai Harn, still relatively undiscovered yet less remote than locations such as Sirinath and Mai Khao.

⬥ *The coast near Bang Tao*

THINGS TO SEE & DO

Diving & watersports

Phuket offers an incredible array of water-based activities to enjoy. While the diving isn't as good as it used to be due to overuse, it is still top-notch. Most operators offer trips to the nearby Similan Islands, day courses, PADI certification and snorkelling. Prices are extremely competitive, but you should check certifications before actually booking anything.

Sea kayaking in Ao Phang-Nga National Park (90 minutes north of Phuket) is another popular option (see pages 80–81). If you're a James Bond fan, you'll appreciate the secluded coves and limestone cliffs made famous in the film *The Man with the Golden Gun*.

For something less strenuous, consider chartering a yacht. Choose your own ship or join one of the trips offered on an authentic Chinese junk moored at Phuket Boat Lagoon.

Golf

There are many good courses for both beginners and advanced players to try during their stay. The following three courses stand out from the rest, and rates are competitive. Always book your round in advance during the high season.

Banyan Tree Club & Laguna @ 34 Moo 4, Srisoonthorn Road, Cherngtalay
@ (0) 7627 0991

Blue Canyon Country Club @ 165 Moo 1, Thepkasattri Road, Thalang
@ (0) 7632 8088

Phuket Country Club @ 80/1 Vichitsongkram Road, Katu @ (0) 7632 9400

Patong

Phuket's red-light district has to be seen once to be believed. Giving Bangkok a run for its money, Patong is a collection of go-go bars, strip shows, cabaret performances and drinking dens that cater to the spicier side in all of us. Some find it sleazy and depressing, others are awed and amused; go and make up your own mind. When it all gets too much, grab a bar stool near the beach and relax with a pint or two.

Sirinath National Park

Located in the northwest corner of Phuket island, this protected national park boasts 90 sq km (35 sq miles) of beautiful forests and beachfront. Snorkellers and divers are drawn by the largest coral reef in shallow water near Phuket, situated around 1.5 km (1 mile) from shore. Try to time your visit between November and February, when it's nesting season for giant leatherback turtles. The park is located close to the airport just off Highway 402.

Spas & treatments

Spa enthusiasts flock to Phuket due to its world-renowned collection of Thai-style spas. Massage and body treatments offered here rank among the world's best. While streetside shopfronts provide great experiences, the truly dedicated speak reverentially about the centres located within Phuket's major resorts. Always book well in advance if you want to be blissfully pampered. The best of the bunch are located at **Banyan Tree resort** (❶ (0) 7632 4374), **Evason** (❶ (0) 7638 1010) and **Hilton Phuket** (❶ (0) 7639 6433).

TAKING A BREAK

Michael's Bar £ ❶ A pleasant place to put into port in central Phuket town. Serves English and other Western food, and is a favourite hangout for resident expats. ⓐ 12 Thanon Takuapa, Phuket town ❶ (0) 7625 6562 ⓦ www.phuket-town.com/michaels ⏰ 12.00–01.00

Patong Seafood Restaurant ££ ❷ There are a number of open-air seafood restaurants along the Patong Beach strip, and this is one of the best. All items on the menu are locally caught, and the variety of cooking styles is impressive. ⓐ 98/2 Thanon Thaweewong, Patong ❶ (0) 7634 1244 ⏰ 08.00–24.00

Boathouse Wine & Grill £££ ❸   Western tourists are dazzled by the Thai and international dishes on offer at this delightful fusion restaurant. While it isn't outdoors, the spacious interiors give the place a welcoming vibe. The cooking school is especially recommended. Grab a cocktail and savour the sunset from your table for two. ⓐ 114 Thanon Patak, Kata ❶ (0) 7633 0557 ⓦ www.boathousephuket.com ⓛ 06.30–23.00

Old Siam £££ ❹   Lovely, open-air, Thai-style restaurant. Go on Wednesdays or Sundays when the Thai buffet and traditional dance display are available. ⓐ Thavorn Palm Beach Hotel, 311 Thanon Patak, Karon ❶ (0) 7639 6090 ⓛ 12.00–15.00, 18.00–23.30

On the Rock £££ ❺   Enjoy spectacular views of Karon Beach as you dine on good-quality Thai food in this pleasant eatery that boasts a scenic deck. Unlike other restaurants of its kind, it isn't all gloss and pretension. Instead, it retains many elements of rustic charm. Great food and simple furnishings make it a good find. ⓐ Marina Phuket Resort, 47 Thanon Karon, Karon ❶ (0) 7633 0625 ⓛ 08.00–23.00

AFTER DARK

Restaurants
The Cliff £££ ❻   This restaurant is part of the large Centara Hotel resort complex, perched above Karon on the way to Patong. The beef is grilled to perfection. Alternatively, tuck into one of the range of Thai curries. ⓐ Centara Karon Resort, 35/37 Moo 1 Thanon Patak, Kata ❶ (0) 7639 6498 ⓦ www.phuket.net/going-out/restaurants/cliff-restaurant.htm ⓛ 18.00–23.00

Ka Jok See £££ ❼   Local players and moneymakers flock to this secret find of a restaurant due to its tasty fusion international/Thai cuisine and intimate interiors. A great place for a quiet, romantic meal. Call for reservations. ⓐ 26 Thanon Takuapa (off Thanon Rasada), Phuket town.

No sign. Look for a screen of hanging plants ☎ (0) 7621 7903
🕐 18.00–24.00, closed Mon

Baan Rim Pa Piano Bar & Restaurant £££ ❽   A long-time favourite with
international visitors, this Thai eatery is everything you want and more.
Views, atmosphere, romance – it's all here. And the excellent food

⬤ *An unusual cargo in a Phuket street*

matches the surroundings perfectly. ⓐ 223 Thanon Prabaramee, Kalim Beach ⓣ (0) 7634 4079 ⓦ www.baanrimpa.com ⓛ 11.30–24.00

Salvatore's Restaurant £££ ❾   The finest Italian food east of Italy. Salvatore serves up great regional Italian cuisine. The desserts are especially tasty. ⓐ 15 Thanon Rasada, Phuket town ⓣ (0) 7622 5958 ⓦ www.salvatorestaurant.com ⓛ 11.30–15.00, 18.00–23.00

Bars
Phuket Bar £ ❿   Rather the Harry Potter of Phuket watering holes, this long-time Patong establishment now lives literally under the stairs of a large disco. No sign, but the doors open at 21.00. ⓐ Under the stairs of the Banana Disco, 124 Thanong Thaweewong, Patong ⓣ (0) 7634 0301 ⓦ www.patongbeachthailand.com/phuketnightlife/live-music-guide/ phuket-bar-in-front-of-pa.shtml ⓛ 21.00–02.00

The Green Man ££ ⓫   Just over the hill from the twin beach resorts of Karon and Kata sits a sprawling English manor house, de facto abode of Phuket's British expat community. Everything is here for the comfort of those away from home. Sunday roasts, holiday parties, evening singalongs, you name it. All in a setting that will warm your heart. ⓐ 82/15 Moo 4, Thanon Patak, southern end of Phuket district ⓣ (0) 7628 0757 ⓦ www.the-green-man.net ⓛ 12.00–whenever

Harry's Steakhouse & Pub ££ ⓬   Patang's best drinking choice is an always-bopping bar offering pints of local brew. Always attracts an international crowd. ⓐ 110/2 Soi Big One, Thanon Thaweewong, Patong ⓦ www.harrys-phuket.com ⓣ (0) 7634 0418 ⓛ 11.00–02.00

Tiger Entertainment ££ ⓭   If you're looking for a raucous night out, then this vast entertainment complex is often the first (or last) point of call. Don't go if you have anything against go-go bars and the people they attract. ⓐ Thanon Bangla, Patong ⓣ (0) 7634 5112 ⓦ www.phuketdir.com/tigerdisco/index.htm ⓛ 12.00–02.00

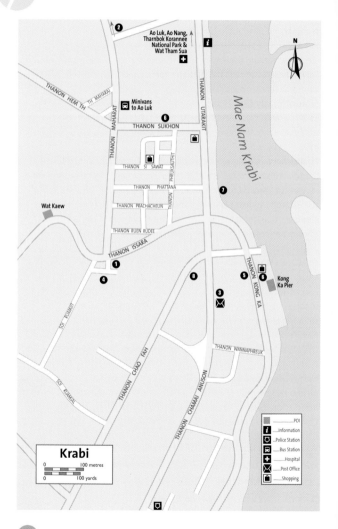

Ao Luk, Ao Nang,
Tharnbok Korannee
National Park &
Wat Tham Sua

THANON HEM TH MAHARAT

THANON MAHARAT

Minivans
to Ao Luk

THANON UTARAKIT

THANON SUKHON

THANON SI SAWAT

THANON PHRUSAUTHIT

THANON PHATTANA

THANON PRACHACHEUN

Wat Kaew

THANON RUEN RUDEE

THANON ISSARA

SOI RUAKUIT

SOI RUAMAI

THANON CHAO FAH

THANON CHAMAI ANUSON

THANON WANNAPHREUK

Mae Nam Krabi

THANON KONG KA

Kong
Ka Pier

Krabi

0	100 metres
0	100 yards

POI
i ....Information
....Police Station
....Bus Station
+ ....Hospital
✉ ....Post Office
....Shopping

Krabi

The town of Krabi itself is far from beautiful. Most pass through on the way to the more stunning offerings at locations such as Koh Phi Phi and Koh Lanta. Package tourists are drawn to the region due to the collection of stunning limestone cliffs that make up the bulk of the local coastline. Be inspired by these beautiful formations on snorkelling day trips or by catching one of the numerous ferries that patrol up and down the coast to island getaways.

Krabi is a great base for budget travellers who are looking to enjoy the trappings of the region but are unwilling to pay the expensive rates at resorts in nearby communities. Ao Nang Beach, which is easily accessible by *songtao* (share taxi), is especially well regarded. To pass straight through Krabi town on the way to other, more notable

⏺ *A Krabi street with distinctive traffic lights*

communities might be tempting, but you would miss out on the inspiring offerings the region has in store.

BEACHES

The beaches around Krabi town are far from inspiring. What makes this resort so spectacular, however, are the number of phenomenal stretches of sand within easy reach. The most convenient beach to get to is Ao Nang, located 22 km (13½ miles) west of the city. While there are other beaches that make this area look pale in comparison, package tourists love Ao Nang due to its easy access to Krabi and the large number of diversions it offers in the form of shops and restaurants. For something a little more secluded and intimate, go 4 km (2½ miles) beyond Ao Nang to the more sedate beach at Hat Noppharat Thara.

One of the best things to do if you're searching for the perfect beach is to join one of the numerous circle-island tours advertised in town. Choose either the four-island cruise that hits Koh Hua Khwan, Koh Poda, Koh Taloo and Tham Phra Nang with beautiful Railay Beach, or the five-island itinerary to Koh Daeng, Koh Hong, Koh Lading, Koh Pakiba and Koh Rai. Both trips offer great snorkelling and nature-viewing opportunities.

THINGS TO SEE & DO

Rock climbing

The limestone cliffs that give this region its distinctive character are also popular with climbers. Many local companies offer full- and half-day courses to novices. Some of the better schools include **Hot Rock** (❶ (0) 7562 1771 ❿ www.railayadventure.com) and **King Climbers** (❶ (0) 7563 7125 ❿ www.railay.com).

Snorkelling & island-hopping

Underwater scenes around Krabi are spectacular. It's well worth getting out of town to find secluded spots to explore the area and its fish-filled viewing spots. Ask your hotel reception or pop into one of the numerous tour agencies located in Ao Nang or Krabi town. Diving is also available, but the best dive sites are located far from the coast. You're better to save your money for easier-access spots near Phuket or Koh Phi Phi.

Tharnbok Korannee National Park

This national preservation zone 46 km (28½ miles) northwest of Krabi is packed with caves, islands and mangrove forests. It can be explored via long-tail boat or sea kayak. Pick up your preferred transport method from the piers at Ban Bho Tho located 7 km (4½ miles) south of Ao Luk.

Wat Tham Sua (Tiger Cave Temple)

Construction has reached a feverish pace to keep up with the demand that currently exists to visit this temple, which is now one of southern Thailand's most famous. People flock here to practise meditation in the prayer hall.

ⓐ East of Krabi on Route 4 🕐 24 hours

🔺 *Ao Nang Beach is one of the most popular near Krabi*

TAKING A BREAK

Gecko House £ ❶   Very comfortable and homely place to enjoy a bite and a relax at midday. ⓐ 1/37 Soi Ruamjit, Krabi town ⓣ (0) 8 0648 5767 ⓛ 07.00–22.00

Ruen Mai £ ❷   Not to be confused with the similar-sounding Ruan Pae, this restaurant offers top-notch local specialities in a lush garden setting. Menus are available in English on request. ⓐ 315/5 Thanon Maharat, Krabi town, about 3 km (2 miles) north of the town centre ⓣ (0) 7563 1797 ⓛ 11.30–22.30

Up 2 You £ ❸   Mr Chai's popular restaurant, bar, guesthouse and internet café. Backpacker central. ⓐ 91 Thanon Utarakit, Krabi town ⓣ (0) 8743 8736 ⓛ 08.30–until last customer

Café Europa ££ ❹   Krabi is hugely popular with the Scandinavian set, and this European café-style restaurant is their locale of choice. Dine on great imported steaks and top it off with a glass of wine from the well-stocked list. ⓐ 9/1 Soi Ruamjit, Krabi town ⓣ (0) 7562 0407 ⓦ http://krabidir.com/cafeeuropa ⓛ 07.00–22.00

AFTER DARK

Restaurants
Kotung £ ❺   If you've ever followed the rule that you should eat where the locals go, then you'll definitely wind up at this cheap Thai eatery with a wide selection of fresh fish and Thai/Chinese dishes. ⓐ 36 Thanon Kong Ka Krabi town ⓣ (0) 7561 1522 ⓛ 11.00–21.00, closed Sun

Night market £ ❻   Not a restaurant name but two markets, these collections of food stalls are the most atmospheric and tastiest places in town to get a bite to eat. ⓐ Thanon Sukhon and Kong Ka, Krabi town ⓛ Dusk–late

Ruan Pae ££ ❼ This floating restaurant boasts a great location and gets a lot of diners as a result. Unfortunately, the food here is not really to be recommended. Stop in for a coffee or beer at midday or on a moonlit night, and enjoy the view. ⓐ Thanon Utarakit, Krabi town ❶ (0) 7561 1956 ❶ 11.30–22.30

Bars

Old West Bar ❶ Come for the cocktails at this cheesily themed (yet fun and festive) bar offering a party almost every night. ⓐ 9/1 Thanon Chao Fah, Krabi town ⓦ www.oldwestbar.claudia-seifert.com ❶ 13.00–02.00

🔺 *A secluded cove at Tham Phra Nang*

Trang

Further south than the better-known province of Krabi, Trang is the newest entrant into the collection of resort developments that lines the Andaman coast. As development hasn't reached epic levels yet, the beaches of Trang are highly rated, featuring less of the litter and pollution often found in other resort communities. Especially popular with middle-class Thais, the city of Trang is used mostly as a transit point for Westerners on their way to the region's sublime islands and nature reserves.

During the high season, a network of ferries transports travellers from Krabi as far down as Malaysia – an increasingly popular option for those who want to see more of the south's spectacular topography.

After the rainy season, surfers flock to Trang's beaches as the surf pounds the sands for a short period of time. Trang in Thai means 'City of Waves', but don't go expecting any Hawaiian-style opportunities.

BEACHES

The most accessible beach to Trang town is Pakmeng, located 40 km (25 miles) west of the town. This beach is only suitable for those looking to sunbathe, as swimming is not advised; swells here can create powerful undertows that would challenge even the strongest swimmers. Slightly north is Hua Hin (not to be confused with the resort of the same name), a delightful bay, famous for its oysters and scattered throughout with limestone outcrops.

For true privacy, head south to the beaches of Hat Chao Mai National Park. Beaches located within this 230-sq km (89-sq mile) park are absolutely flawless. Private development is controlled in this region, meaning that some days will see only you and your bottle of sunscreen populating the area. Beaches to be found here include (from north to south) Hat San, Hat Yong Ling, Hat Yao and Hat Chao Mai. You can stay overnight in the park by getting a bed at the park headquarters. Cabins are simple, with rooms sleeping up to eight. Alternatively, you can set up tent under the casuarina trees on the shore nearby.

◯ *A monument to the King in Trang*

THINGS TO SEE & DO

Hat Chao Mai National Park

This 230-sq km (89-sq mile) collection of islands and forests is what you came to Thailand dreaming of. Wildlife spotters will relish the chance to see otters, dugongs and the wild boar for which the region is famous. If you have the time, try to plan an overnight stay at the cabins located at the park headquarters.

From Trang city, take road 4046 west. At the 30-km (18-mile) post, turn left onto road 4162 south to Pakmeng Beach. Continue 7 km (4 miles) beyond Pakmeng to park headquarters **(o) 7521 3260** www.dnp.go.th reserve@dnp.go.th

Khuen Keng (Kuan Khang) Hot Springs

A beautiful waterfall, naturally heated to a constant temperature of 60°C (140°F). Bring your bathing costume if you want to take a dip. No public transport is available, so you will have to find your own way of getting here.

Trang Road, 2 km (1½ miles) east of the Hat Yao turnoff 24 hours

Snorkelling

Numerous day-trip operators take visitors to the beautiful waters around Koh Ngai and Koh Rok. Pop into any of the agencies that offer packages to plan your adventure; you'll find them located near the pier of every major town along the coast of Trang province. If you haven't brought your own mask and fins, be sure to rent them before you get on board.

TAKING A BREAK

Mainland

Baan Ko Lan £ For the real *ahahn chao trang* (Trang breakfast), here or anywhere else in town, the key is to get there *early*. People line up at 06.00. By 08.00 the best stuff is gone, and it's all over by 09.30. Take it to heart. ⓐ Thanon Huai Yot, near Soi 7 next to the minibus stop, Trang city. Not marked in English, so ask someone ⓣ (0) 7522 2925 ⓛ 06.00–10.00

Lay Trang Resort ££ Pleasant outdoor restaurant specialising in fresh seafood and Thai specialities and boasting a patio area. ⓐ 54/22 Moo 4, Maifad ⓣ (0) 7527 4027 ⓦ www.laytrang.com ⓔ laytrangresort@ yahoo.com ⓛ 08.00–22.00

Islands
Rubber Tree Bungalow ££ Eat among the branches of a rubber tree in this peaceful restaurant on stilts. The food is average, but the atmosphere is sublime. ⓐ Ko Muk (Muk Island) ⓣ (0) 7520 3284 ⓛ 12.00–22.00

⬤ *A view from the pier, Trang*

AFTER DARK

Restaurants
Mainland
Haadyao Nature Resort ££ The speciality here is chemical-free fish, prawns and other seafood, and completely organic vegetables. Fresh, healthy and very, very tasty. ⓐ Baan Chao Mai ⓣ (0) 8 1894 6936 ⓦ www.trangsea.com ⓛ 07.30–21.00

Islands
Kradan Beach Resort ££ A lovely place to dine or to stay. ⓐ Koh Kradan (Kradan Island) ⓣ (0) 8 1495 9621 ⓦ www.kradanbeachresort.com ⓛ 07.00–22.00

Thapwarin Resort ££ A wide variety of traditional Thai and Western fare, served under the trees or in the open-air restaurant. ⓐ Koh Ngai (Ngai Island) ⓣ (0) 7522 0139 ⓦ www.thapwarin.com ⓛ 07.30–22.00

Koh Hai Fantasy Resort & Spa £££ Take the ferry to Koh Ngai to enjoy great seafood at this highly recommended resort hotel. ⓐ Koh Ngai (Ngai Island) ⓣ (0) 7521 0317 ⓛ 07.30–22.30

⦿ *The idyllic coast of Koh Phi Phi*

EXCURSIONS
Out & about

EXCURSIONS

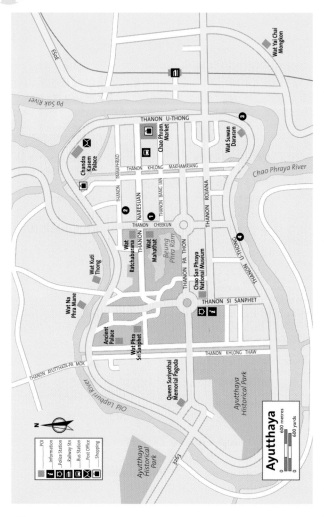

Ayutthaya

0 ——————— 600 metres
0 ——————— 600 yards

Wat Yai Chai Mongkon

Chao Phrom Market

THANON U-THONG

Wat Suwan Dararam

Pa Sak River

Chao Phraya River

Chandra Kasem Palace

THANON PAMAPHRAO

THANON KHLONG MAKHAMRIANG

THANON NARESUAN

THANON BANG IAN

THANON ROJANA

THANON CHEEKUN

THANON U THONG

Wat Kuti Thong

Wat Ratchaburana

Wat Mahathat

Beung Phra Ram

Chao San Phraya National Museum

THANON PA THON

Wat Na Phra Mane

Ancient Palace

Wat Phra Sri Sanphet

THANON SI SANPHET

Queen Suriyothai Memorial Pagoda

THANON KHLONG THAW

THANON AYUTTHATA-PA MOK

Old Lopburi River

Ayutthaya Historical Park

Ayutthaya Historical Park

N

- POI
- Information
- Police Station
- Railway Stn
- Bus Station
- Post Office
- Shopping

From Bangkok

Ayutthaya

As the capital of the Kingdom of Siam from circa 1350 to 1760, Ayutthaya was a glittering showpiece until it was destroyed by the Burmese in 1767. Over 33 kings called Ayutthaya home, with its peak occurring in the 18th century when the region could boast multiple palaces and more than 400 temples. A 15-month siege by the Burmese ended the town's 'Golden Age' and resulted in its almost complete destruction.

🚆 There are 15 trains a day that make the trip from Bangkok's Hua Lampong Station. Alternatively, buses depart every 20 minutes from Bangkok's Northern Bus Terminal. The journey takes approximately an hour and a half.

THINGS TO SEE & DO

Ancient Palace
Formerly the main palace of the capital, it was destroyed by the Burmese in 1767; just the original foundations remain.
ⓐ Northwest section of old city ⏰ 08.00–18.00

Chandra Kasem Palace
Now a branch of the National Museum, this former palace holds a collection of artefacts that date back to between the 13th and 17th centuries.
ⓐ Northeast section of old city ⓦ www.thailandmuseum.com
⏰ 09.00–12.00, 13.00–16.00 Wed–Sun ❶ Admission charge

Chao San Phraya National Museum
Packed with treasures, the museum – the second largest in Thailand – boasts an impressive collection of Buddhas and religious objects.
ⓐ Thanon Rojana ☎ (0) 3524 1587 ⓦ www.thailandmuseum.com
⏰ 09.00–16.00 Wed–Sun ❶ Admission charge

Wat Mahathat

Built in 1384, this is the most atmospheric of all the ruins on-site and is a popular place from which to enjoy the sunset.

ⓐ Thanon Sikhun 🕒 08.00–18.00 ❶ Admission charge

Wat Na Phra Mane

This relatively intact temple features a magnificently carved black stone Buddha that dates back to the Dvaravati period (6th–11th centuries).

ⓐ North of Ancient Palace 🕒 08.00–17.00 ❶ Admission charge

Wat Phra Sri Sanphet

Originally the private chapel of the king, this reconstructed temple was destroyed by fire in 1767 by the Burmese invaders.

ⓐ South of Ancient Palace 🕒 08.00–17.00 ❶ Admission charge

Wat Yai Chai Mongkon

Look for the massive gold *chedi* (bell-shaped tower) at the top of this *wat* to find this beautiful temple. Founded in the 14th century, it is one of the oldest in the city.

ⓐ Southwest of train station 🕒 08.00–18.00 ❶ Admission charge

TAKING A BREAK

Siam Restaurant £ ❶   Located just across the street from Wat Mahathat, this air-conditioned eatery offers a variety of dishes. Great for when your legs start to get weary with all your explorations.

ⓐ 11/3 Thanon Pratuchai ❶ (0) 3521 1070 🕒 10.00–22.00

Ruean Rojjana Thai Restaurant ££ ❷   Respectable and attractively priced Thai cuisine, directly across from the ruins of Wat Ratchaburana. A perfect place to get out of the midday heat. ⓐ 22/13 Thanon Maharat ❶ (0) 3532 3765 ⓦ www.rueanrojjana.com 🕒 10.00–21.00

● Wat Phra Sri Sanphet

AFTER DARK

Restaurants

Pae Krung Kao ££ ❸ While away the hours at this restaurant located right on the riverside on a collection of floating piers. This is what every Thai restaurant should look and feel like, complete with acoustic musicians playing 1960s standards, fantastic stir-fries and views of the khlongs and passing long-tails. Sheer bliss. ⓐ 4 Moo 2, Thanon U-Thong ⓣ (0) 3524 1555 ⓛ 07.00–22.00

Ruan Rub Rong ££ ❹ For something a little different, grab a table at this riverside restaurant. Dinner cruises are available for groups by prior arrangement only. ⓐ 13/1–2 Thanon U-Thong ⓣ (0) 3524 3090 ⓦ www.ruanrubrong.net ⓛ 10.00–22.00

From Pattaya

Koh Samet

Further south from Pattaya and located a short ferry hop from the coastal town of Ban Phe is the sedate island of Koh Samet. With crystal-clear waters, powder-sand beaches and 14 secluded coves, it's a far cry from the all-night circus that is Pattaya. While development has reached the island, it isn't as frenetic as in other resorts due to the island's status as part of a national park system. If you're looking for a beach resort that's within striking distance of Bangkok or Pattaya and will give you a real taste of Thai paradise, then you've come to the right place.

 From Pattaya, the easiest way to get to Koh Samet is by taking the bus to Ban Phe Bus Station pier, where you can catch the ferry over to the island.

THINGS TO SEE & DO

As Koh Samet has overtaken Pattaya as the chic place for a weekend break for residents of the capital, it is brimming with diving operators and watersports activities. There is very little to see culturally in this resort community; visitors come for fun and frolicking in the clear water.

Good dive sites are located far from the resort itself, making it a secondary choice for true pros, but it's a good place for novices who just want to try diving for the first time. Generally, visitors just go to Koh Samet to splash around and enjoy themselves. Most rental establishments offer a variety of items such as boogie boards and inner tubes.

Koh Samet is part of a national park, so beaches tend to be well maintained and lack the litter and chaos of other east-coast resorts. And, if you like a laid-back drink and a chance to watch the sunset, then you've come to the right place as this is not a party-all-night kind of destination. If you do want some nightlife and action, though, head over to Hat Sai Kaew, the beach development that is experiencing the biggest boom in construction.

❶ As Koh Samet is a unit of Thailand's national park system, an admission charge is collected for each person landing on the island. Adults are charged 200 baht each.

TAKING A BREAK

Mobile Noodle Stand £ In some Western cities, there are mobile sandwich stands for workers on the go – this is the Thai equivalent. Tuck into a yummy bowl of noodles or other fare by hailing any of the many mobile restaurants that move from place to place anywhere in Thailand. **🕐** Early morning to late, late at night.

◯ *One of Koh Samet's white beaches*

Jep's Bungalows ££ This good breakfast and lunch spot serves great baked goods in the morning. Get there early to enjoy the smell of rising dough. ⓐ Ao Hin Khok, south of Hat Sai Kaew ⓣ (0) 3864 4112 ⓦ www.jepbungalow.com ⓛ 07.00–23.00

AFTER DARK

Restaurants

Naga Bar £ Food is served here, but most clients just pull up and grab a beer (or three) at this laid-back drinking den. ⓐ Ao Hin Khok ⓛ 07.00–02.00

Moo Ban Talay ££ The beach near it may be a little downbeat, but the food served at this minimally chic restaurant is worth going out of your way for. ⓐ Ao Noi Na ⓣ (0) 3864 4251 ⓛ 07.00–22.00

Bars

Raebang Bar Nibbles and beers are served up at this convenient bar near the ferry piers. A good place to head for if you are waiting for a connection to the mainland or a nearby island. ⓐ Na Dan Pier ⓛ 07.30–02.00

Reggae Bar Bob Marley lives at this bar and its siblings that seem to be a standard part of every beach resort in Thailand. Cool Reggae sounds on the deck, and karaoke inside if you go that way. ⓐ Ao Hin Khok ⓛ 12.00–02.00

Silver Sand Bar Koh Samet's version of a nightclub is this buzzy drinking and dancing venue that stays open until the wee hours. The music isn't exactly cutting edge, but it fits the retro atmosphere here. ⓐ Ao Phai ⓣ (0) 6530 2417 ⓛ 13.00–02.00

From Koh Samui

Koh Phangan

This is an island where you can still find secluded beaches and cheap beach huts that cater to backpackers as they bop their way around Southeast Asia. Package tourists are a rare sight here, so, if you're looking for 5-star options, it's best to stick to Koh Samui. Those in search of a full mind-body experience will appreciate the island's meditation, yoga and massage centres. If you need any little luxuries, bring them with you, as many amenities are unavailable.

 Ferries run regularly to Koh Phangan from Big Buddha and Nathon Pier on Koh Samui. Extra services are usually put on in time for the full moon events.

THINGS TO SEE & DO

Diving & snorkelling
Other resorts have better diving and snorkelling sites, but there are still plenty of diversions here if you want to see life under the sea. Head to the northwest of the island to witness the best displays of aquatic life. There are plenty of operators offering diving and snorkelling rentals along the coast. Bring your own masks and snorkels if you want to ensure quality.

MIND, BODY & SPIRIT
Traditional yoga and massage centres abound on Koh Phangan. Enjoy an alternative treatment or take a course to learn how to do it yourself. Hat Chaophao and Haad Rin are packed with practitioners – just see one you like and pop in.

🔺 *Palm trees fringe the shore on Koh Phangan*

Jungle hikes

Take the trek up to the top of the island's biggest mountain, Khao Ra. Trails are well marked and easy to traverse. On clear days, you can see as far as Koh Tao. Guides are recommended. Find available guides by consulting signs and operators located near Thong Sala Pier.

Wat Khao Tham

Once occupied by a lone monk for over a decade, this cave temple is a peaceful place for a spot of meditation. It's located along the coast in Surat Thani, and you can get there by flagging a share taxi. There are no set hours, but ten-day retreats are offered by a resident couple in the second half of each month.

Waterfalls

Four waterfalls in the interior of the island draw crowds to their flowing drops every year. A favourite with the Thai royal family, they were especially loved by Rama V, who visited 18 times over the course of his reign. The waterfalls can be reached by hiring a guide or flagging a share taxi.

TAKING A BREAK

Mr K £ The trance set love this good Thai greasy spoon due to its cheap prices and 'we never close' policy. A great place to head for if you get the munchies in the wee hours. ⓐ Haad Rin ⓣ (0) 7737 5470 ⓛ 24 hrs

The Sweet Café Bakery ££ Great breakfast and lunch spot serving simple treats such as muffins and home-made yogurt. ⓐ Thong Sala ⓣ (0) 8 7275 6131 ⓛ 07.00–21.00

The Village Green ££ Popular with backpackers, this elegant teak house acts as a form of information hut where visitors swap stories, tips and travellers' tales. The international/Thai food enjoys an excellent reputation – especially the breakfast menu. ⓐ Hat Chaophao ⓣ (0) 7734 9217 ⓛ 10.00–24.00

AFTER DARK

Restaurants

Om Ganesh ££ Tasty Indian eatery with fantastic curries. ⓐ Haad Rin, Main Road, near ferry pier ⓣ (0) 7737 5123 ⓛ 08.00–23.00

Al Arena £££ Outstanding Italian food, when you're ready for a treat. ⓐ Haad Rin ⓣ (0) 8 7189 2236 ⓛ 17.00–23.00

Bars

The Mason's Arms It's a new trend – British-style public houses in Thai beach resorts. Check it out. ⓐ Thong Sala ⓣ (0) 7723 8526 ⓦ www.themasonsarms.in.th ⓛ 10.30–01.00

Pirates Set on a re-created pirate ship that juts out from a cliff, this always-popular bar is packed with revellers drawn to its crazy architecture and regular full moon parties. ⓐ Hat Chaophao ⓣ (0) 4728 6064 ⓛ 20.30–02.00

FULL MOON PARTIES

Koh Samui used to be party central for the legendary full moon events that packed its beaches every month. As development has taken over this once remote destination, the party has moved to nearby Koh Phangan. Over 10,000 flock to the beach at Haad Rin East to live it up under the bright evening sky, and the festivities can last all night. For details see ⓦ www.kohphangan.com

From Krabi & Phuket

Ao Phang-Nga

Part of Thailand's national park system, this beautiful bay area is exactly what many travellers think of when they dream of Thai paradise. Beautiful beaches, intimate villages and dramatic limestone cliffs greet the sapphire ocean, to the sublime content of all who visit. Choose to flop on the beach or get active by renting a kayak to explore the hidden coves and crannies that make up this beautiful corner of the world.

THINGS TO SEE & DO

Island tours
There are numerous operators that offer tours of the island just offshore of Ao Phang-Nga National Park. One of the most popular destinations is Khao Tapu, otherwise known as 'James Bond Island' due to its use as the location for filming Scaramanga's lair in the film *The Man with the Golden Gun*. Boats can be chartered from the piers at Tha Dan, approximately 8.5 km (5¼ miles) south of Phang-Nga town.

AFTER DARK

Restaurants
Bismilla £ Good southern Thai specialities with a strong emphasis on seafood. Budget travellers will appreciate the cheap prices.
ⓐ Thanon Petchikasem, Phang-Nga town 🕐 12.00–22.00

> ### VEGETARIAN FESTIVAL
> If you like your greens, then make a beeline for this national park region in October when meat-free dishes are celebrated in the area's restaurants. A plethora of menu items featuring regional produce is served up to the masses during this festive period.

Mr Satay ££ Great Malaysian satay for those who are looking for something other than traditional Thai food. ⓐ 184 Thanon Petchikasem, Phang-Nga town ⓣ (0) 7641 1322 ⓦ www.mrsatay.com ⓛ 10.00–22.00

⬤ *Khao Tapu, familiar to James Bond fans*

Koh Phi Phi

If you saw any of the coverage relating to the 2004 tsunami, you will know that Phi Phi was badly hit. However, resconstruction has now been completed, and the island is back to its old self. It remains one of Thailand's most beautiful destinations, drawing fans of nature and party lifestyle alike to its shores.

Ⓝ Regular ferries make the trip twice daily from both Krabi and Phuket. From Krabi, allow more than 2 hours to make the trip, and just a bit less from Phuket. Speedboats can travel faster, but at correspondingly higher cost.

THINGS TO SEE & DO

Diving & snorkelling
There are heaps of operators offering visits to the reefs that surround Phi Phi. Professionals rave about the clear water and shipwrecks that make the region so spectacular. Always check the operator's certifications before booking.

Long-tail tours
See more of the island by joining a long-tail tour of the region. Stop off at Koh Mai Phai (Bamboo Island), Phi Phi Leh, Monkey Bay and Wang Long beach on a day trip that combines great views with eco-friendly snorkelling. For the best tour, try booking with **Adventure Club** (Ⓣ (0) 8 1895 1334).

Rock climbing
Phi Phi's cliffs are heaven-sent for fans of rock climbing. The views from the top make the effort well worth the sweat that goes into it. The best climbs can be found at Hin Taak and Ton Sai Tower. Note that there are no operators offering equipment rental or guides on Koh Phi Phi. If you want to enjoy the challenge, join a day trip with one of the outfits on Krabi's Railay Beach or rent your equipment through them.

⬥ *One of Phi Phi's perfect beaches*

TAKING A BREAK

Garden Home Restaurant £ A few minutes' walk from the bustle of the tourist village, Mr Bao's Garden Home is a peaceful place to nurse your morning-after hangover or just to relax. Very cheerful and friendly, with excellent breakfast and Thai or Western food all day long. ⓐ Across from Phitarom Resort, on the way to the viewpoint ⓣ (0) 8 1894 3835 ⓛ 07.00–02.00

AFTER DARK

Restaurants
Papaya ££ A well-established and popular eatery in Phi Phi's 'Reggae Bar Ghetto', this reasonably priced restaurant serves up incredible Thai food. Often crowded in the evening and late-night party hours. ⓐ Tourist Village ⓛ 12.00–03.00

Bars
Reggae Bar A hit before the tsunami, this popular bar was rebuilt quickly and is now back to normal. Regular shows feature *muay thai* (kickboxing) and ladyboy displays. ⓐ Tourist Village ⓛ 07.00–02.00

⦿ *A statue's head entwined by tree roots at Ayutthaya*

Food & drink

The food of Thailand is delicious and incredibly diverse. Spices give every meal a kick, with flavours dependent upon the region where the dish comes from. Both meat-eaters and vegetarians will appreciate the wealth of items on every menu, ranging from commonly known treats such as *Pad Thai* (stir-fried rice noodles, egg, bean sprouts, shrimp, peanuts and seasonings) through to more exotic tastes involving grilled insects. And the wealth of locally grown exotic fruits will provide a refreshing tonic on hot days when a sweet, juicy treat is exactly what you're craving.

Each of the four geographic zones of Thailand – northern, central, southern and northeastern (also known as Isaan) – produces its own distinctive cuisine. You can get dishes from each zone across the country, but you'll find that your meal will reflect the native region the kitchen chef hails from. If the cook is from the south but you're staying in Pattaya, start scanning the menu for southern treats in order to enjoy a good meal.

Unlike in the West, the range of items available may not reflect the skill of the staff. Some of the best places to eat specialise in serving just a single dish, but they do it very well. Streetside and market eating is also recommended, as these small sellers often provide the most memorable taste sensations. When selecting market food, always ensure that the seller is hygienic and cooks food thoroughly. You don't want a dose of dodgy tummy with your chicken and rice.

RESTAURANT TIPPING

Tipping in restaurants is not expected but is becoming more common in the bigger resort towns. Many feel this is ruining Thailand's service culture by encouraging locals to expect extra money. The decision is really yours. Note that service charges are now commonly being added to bills, but these charges are usually not passed down to the poorly paid staff. So any extra you want to give for good service will be appreciated.

Thais eat at all hours, and snacking is common, which is why street sellers are so prevalent throughout the country. Meals are grabbed later than northern Europeans might be used to on account of the humidity and higher temperatures.

NORTHERN CUISINE

Thailand's mountainous north is cooler than the rest of the country, a fact that is reflected in its food options and delicacies. Vegetables thrive in these conditions. Thus, vegetarian cuisine is especially strong in this region, with roots and herbs used in many recipes.

Rice is an important staple with every meal; it is often a glutinous variety, which allows locals to use their hands when eating. You'll often find rice dishes served with a selection of dipping sauces. To enjoy the taste, roll the rice in your right hand and dip it into the condiment of your choice.

Popular dishes that hail from the north include the beloved *Som Tam* (green papaya salad) and soups flavoured with bitter and/or sour herbs. Noodles are served frequently by northerners, often brought over from neighbouring regions such as Yunnan (China) and Burma.

Pork is the favoured meat for residents and is served up as often as possible. Sausages made from pork meat are especially delicious from here, often spiced with chillies, garlic and lemon grass to give a unique taste sensation.

Curries from the north tend to be much weaker and thinner than southern varieties and are often sweetened using popular fruits such as jackfruit or banana for a sweet and spicy combination.

If you can try only one meal, make sure to tuck into a *khan toke* dinner, which means 'bowl on low table'. This meal is a sampler plate of the best the region has to offer, served in relaxed surroundings as you kneel before the food placed in front of you. A real experience to be savoured!

CENTRAL CUISINE

The Central Plains draw influences from across the country due to the presence of the capital city within their confines. Thais from all over the nation have moved to Bangkok, bringing their local flavours and traditions with them. Despite this, a central cuisine does exist and has given Thai food some of its best-known dishes.

Tom Yam, arguably one of the most popular items on any restaurant menu, hails from the Central Plains. A hot and sour soup, it's available pretty much everywhere in the country due to its status as a hit item with international tourists. Also beloved are items with a Chinese twist, including clay pot dishes and anything involving tofu or ground pork.

The region's talent for growing rice is reflected in the plethora of items served that include this staple in the recipe. Most Thais agree that rice grown here is the best available, especially jasmine rice. To truly enjoy the rice to its fullest, order another local favourite to go with it –

⬤ *Seafood rules on Koh Phangan*

kaeng khieo wan (Thai green curry). Alternatively, grab an omelette served with chilli sauce for those nights when you're craving something simple yet tasty.

SOUTHERN CUISINE

As home to Thailand's Muslim community, the south reflects its population by using pork a lot less than other areas of the country. Seafood is king in these parts due to the region's abundant coastline and access to the sea. Often these ocean morsels will be prepared very simply – usually steamed or lightly fried – to take full advantage of the delicate flavours.

If you have a dodgy stomach, be warned: southerners like their food fire-alarm hot. Almost everything will be served with chillies, so, if you have an aversion to spicy foods, let your waiter know immediately. Coconut milk is used frequently to counteract the heat of the spices. The milk thickens curries and is also served as a cooling side dish. Cashew nuts and pineapple juice are also employed to sweeten recipes. Yellow curries involving fish stock and green papaya are a favourite in these parts, flavoured with turmeric and coconut milk to give them the bright hue from which they take their name.

NORTHEASTERN (ISAAN) CUISINE

The cuisine of the northeast is highly regarded, yet often shunned by Westerners due to its exotic ingredients. The region itself is one of the poorest in Thailand, and residents have often had to make do with whatever they could get their hands on to survive. Don't be surprised to see creatures such as grasshoppers, beetles, frogs and snakes on Isaan menus – usually roasted or grilled. These items are favourite streetside snacks in the Patpong region of Bangkok, as most of the bar girls who work the streets in the red-light district are from this part of the country.

While fish dishes are popular, they tend to feature river fish varieties rather than seafood or ocean catches. This is due to the geographic makeup of Isaan and its proximity to the Mekong River regions.

⬤ *Lime juice is just one of the many fruit drinks available in Thailand*

Herbs in Isaan dishes are used copiously to give basic staples a kick of taste and to help make a pot of food go further. Glutinous rice is also used, as it tends to fill stomachs faster.

DRINKS

Coffee is a hit with Thais, especially in the growing regions of the south. You will find coffee bars throughout this part of the country serving local beans and/or *chai* (tea) with condensed milk and sugar. If you like your hot drinks black, then specify this before you order.

Also popular are fruit drinks made with exotic, locally grown varieties. If it grows, is sweet and can be eaten, then it will be transformed into a juice, smoothie or ice-shave faster than you can peel an orange. It's a great, natural way to cool down after a long day on the beach.

Alcohol is readily available – and Thais love to drink. Drunkenness is frowned upon, but it can be hard to avoid getting a little tipsy when a bottle of beer costs a fraction of what it does at home. Popular beer brands include Singha, Leo and Chang. Rice whisky is also a hit, especially among the working classes.

Menu decoder

In Thailand, many menus are printed in both Thai and English due to the number of foreign visitors who arrive every year. Some regions may also offer menus in Scandinavian languages, French and Spanish. If you can, try to avoid anywhere that prints multilingual menus, as their food will cater to international palates and won't be as authentic (or tasty) as that in hole-in-the-wall locations. When in doubt, point to what you like the look of.

Chaa Tea, usually served with condensed milk and sugar.

Durian Pungent fruit in season during June and July. Foreigners often complain it smells horrible.

Farang Guava (not to be confused with the Thai term for foreigner or 'white man').

Gaeng Ped Curried dish.

Gek Huey Chrysanthemum juice.

Jackfruit Large, thorned fruit with a tangy centre.

Kaafae Coffee.

Kaafae Dam Black coffee.

Kaeng Jeut Broth-style soup often eaten by those feeling under the weather. The taste is mild, usually flavoured with a dash of soy sauce or fish paste.

Kaeng Khiao-Waan Sweet, green curry flavoured with coconut. A favourite with Western palates.

Kaeng Matsaman Southern curry favoured by the Muslim community, made with chicken or beef and turmeric, cloves, cinnamon, cardamom, chilli and the ubiquitous tamarind.

Kaeng Panaeng Red curry with peanuts.

Kaeng Tai Plaa Spicy fish curry with a thick sauce flavoured with turmeric.

Kai Phat Khing Chicken with ginger.

Kai Phat Met Mamuang Himaphaan Chicken in a fried chilli and cashew sauce.

Kai Thawt Fried chicken.

Khanom Dessert.

Khanom Jiin Naam Yaa Southern yellow curry, usually made with fresh fish and served over wheat noodles.

Khao Rice.

Khao Miaw Sticky rice.

Khao Phat Fried rice.

Khao Soi Northern curried soup.

Khao Yam Breakfast southern style, consisting of rice, bean sprouts, coconut, chilli, shrimp, lemon grass, lime and a tamarind sauce.

Kluay Thawt Fried bananas.

Krueang Kiang Side salad.

Kuaytiaw Rice noodles.

Kuaytiaw Naam Noodles served in meat stock (usually beef or chicken) with cabbage and coriander.

Kuaytiaw Pad Khee Mao Rice noodles fried with chilli, basil and garlic.

Kuaytiaw Rad Na Sen-Yai Rice noodles in a thick gravy with vegetables and meat (usually pork or chicken).

Kung Chup Paeng Thawt Shrimp fried in a batter. Something like Japanese tempura.

Larb Spicy beef or chicken with a mint and lime marinade.

Malakaw Papaya.

Mangosteen Purple, hard-skinned fruit with tasty pale pink segments.

Maphrao Coconut.

Muu Nam Tok Isaan-style starter salad served with roasted rice powder and grilled pork.

Naam Khan Freshly squeezed juice.

Neua Phat Naam-Man Hawy Beef in oyster sauce. Usually found in Chinese establishments.

Pad Noodle dish made with shrimp, eggs, bean sprouts, lime, peanuts and (sometimes) chicken.

Paw Pia Egg rolls.

Phat Hoey Lai Nam Phrik Pao Clams with a roast chilli paste and basil sauce.

Phrik Naam Plaa Fish sauce with fried chillies – Thailand's favourite condiment.

Polamai Fruit.

Puu Phat Pong Karil Stir-fried crab with curry powder, often served with egg.

Roti Fried bread, often found in the south, usually served with curries.

Sapparot Pineapple.

Satay Charcoal-grilled beef, chicken or pork skewered

on a bamboo stick and served with a peanut-coconut sauce.

Som Orange.

Som Tam Spicy green papaya salad.

Taeng Moh Watermelon.

Tamarind Exotically spicy fruit eaten fresh or candied.

Thawt Deep-fried.

Tod Man Pla Fish cakes fried in a sweet honey sauce. Often prepared with local vegetables and served in a banana leaf.

Tom Yang Goong/Tom Yam Goong Hot and sour shrimp soup.

Yam Starter salad. Usually featuring a sweet and sour taste combination.

Yam Pla Dook Foo Fried catfish salad.

Yam Tua Plu Winged bean salad.

Yam Woon-Sen Clear noodle salad made from mung beans, coriander, chillies, lime juice, shrimp and (sometimes) pork.

🌑 *A dish of* Pad

Shopping

Thailand offers a wealth of ways to part you from your cash. A visit to this country of crafts will certainly do damage to your wallet as you will be tempted by the extremely competitive prices for many items compared to what you would pay back home. Haggling is expected in all but the fanciest of shops, so, if you see something you like, prepare to bargain hard. Other than in shopping malls, cash is often the only method of payment accepted. Come prepared with currency if you plan on making purchases.

ANTIQUES

Real antiques are hard to find except in specialist shops in Bangkok. Most 'old' items will be reproductions using ancient techniques. If you are unsure about an item's authenticity, ask the seller. Popular antique purchases include lacquerware, celadon pottery and Buddha figures.

🔺 *A wickerwork stall*

Permits will be required if you plan to export any authentic antique, especially if it is a Buddha image. Your seller should be able to assist you with export information and paperwork.

CLOTHING

Sizes in Thailand are exceptionally small, so you may find that the cool outfit you see hanging on a rack won't go around your thigh, even if it is marked XXL. Depending on where you purchase clothes, quality will vary. Street fashions bought at market stalls will look fun, but may not survive the first wash. Always check seams and stitching to ensure workmanship. Western sizes can best be found in Bangkok, so, if you are in need of some new threads, try to wait until you make a stop in the capital.

COUNTERFEIT GOODS

Once available on almost every street corner, counterfeit goods are no longer the ubiquitous items they once were. Sure, you will find sellers mutter words like 'Real Rolex' or 'Louis Vuitton' when you pass them by, but it isn't like it used to be. Pressure from Western nations has forced the Thai government to crack down on cheap, knock-off goods. Night markets are the best place to head for if you want a cheap bag or watch. If you don't see what you're looking for, ask around and someone will be bound to know where to direct you. Quality varies, so look at a variety of items to compare detail. After all, a fake will make you feel smug, but a bad fake will just make you look cheap.

GEMS

If you do your research, you can pick up amazing gems for a steal. Unfortunately, many disreputable sellers know this and will do their best to take advantage of you at every opportunity. The best buys are in sapphires and rubies, as these stones are native to Thailand and the surrounding region. Emeralds are also available, but are not as good a deal, as they have to be imported. When choosing a gem dealer, avoid the many scams that involve a taxi or *tuk-tuk* driver taking you to a 'good shop they know', as they will be getting a commission for their efforts. If you want to stay safe, choose your gems from one of the shopping centres in Bangkok. You'll be paying top baht, but you'll know you're getting the real thing.

LACQUERWARE

Trays, boxes and containers are available at market stalls and speciality shops. While quality is high, keep your baht in your wallet if you have any plans to go to Vietnam, as items from that country are cheaper and better crafted.

MARKETS

Every resort and town in Thailand has a market, usually selling a combination of food items, souvenirs, clothing and electronics. Many markets are open at night, as daytime temperatures sap locals of their haggling energies. Expect to bargain for anything you decide to purchase. The best market of them all is located at Chatuchak, outside Bangkok. Only open on weekends, it's the best of the bunch, with thousands of stalls to choose from. Crowds can get chaotic, and pickpocketing is rife, so keep an eye on your belongings at all times. Floating markets located west of the capital are also fun, and are usually included as stops on day trips from the city.

SILKS

Thai silk is justifiably raved about, so it may come as a surprise to learn that the industry almost died out a few decades ago. Many regard the

HAGGLING ETIQUETTE

If you start the haggling process you will be expected to buy the item at the end of your battle, so be sure you really want something before you start the process, unless you want to seriously anger the locals.

TAXES

A standard VAT of 7 per cent is applied to all goods purchased in Thai restaurants and shops. Some stores offer a refund service; a minimum purchase of 5,000 baht + VAT is required. Look for the VAT refund sticker in the window of the boutique to see if they operate the service. Refunds can be collected at the VAT Refund Tourist Offices in the Bangkok and Phuket airports when you leave the country.

mysterious ex-CIA operative Jim Thompson to be the man who helped revive admiration for Thai silk back in the 1960s. The best stuff is hand-woven (not machine-made) and will be more expensive as a result. Purchase it in fabric form, or buy scarves, blouses, cushion covers and more. For the finest examples, Jim Thompson stores located across the country in all major resort areas are a good (if expensive) source.

SILVERWARE & CUTLERY

Perhaps surprisingly, Thailand is an excellent place to purchase fine silverware and stainless steel cutlery. You can pick up single pieces or entire services presented in a wooden box. The best items are hand-wrought in a variety of simple designs. Finishings are neat as well, often featuring just a curl at the end of the handle or a plain square-cut. Shell-like patterns and fussy edges are shunned in favour of elegant minimalism, perfectly matching the Zen-like interiors found in Thailand's higher-end interior shops.

Children

Thais love children and will make a fuss of them whenever allowed. Bringing a child with you will ensure smiles flashed your way wherever you go. However, Thai children are also expected to be very well behaved. If your tot is prone to tantrums, you may want to keep them at home on fussy days.

The Thai sun is baking hot and can affect sensitive skin even on overcast days. Take high-SPF sunscreen wherever you go. It is best to purchase this in advance of your trip, as good-quality brands can be difficult to find and/or very expensive in Thailand.

The following are some recommended child-friendly attractions that will help keep the kids happily amused for hours or even days.

AMUSEMENT & WATER PARKS

Suan Siam (Siam Park)

Cool the kids off with a visit to Bangkok's favourite water park. Packed with waterslides, swimming pools and lazy rivers, Suan Siam will cool both your body and your temper down – a godsend during the sweltering hot season. The park is located in Bangkapi, about 30 minutes east of the capital.

ⓐ 101 Thanon Sukhapibarn 2, Bangkapi ⓣ (0) 2919 7200
ⓦ www.siamparkcity.com ⓛ 10.00–18.00 Mon–Fri, 09.00–19.00 Sat & Sun ⓝ Bus: 168 from Victory Monument ⓘ Admission charge

MUSEUMS

Children's Discovery Museum

An activity and learning centre packed with games and exhibits galore. Everything is hands-on, including the live animal exhibits. Try to avoid weekday mornings, when the place is packed out by school groups.

ⓐ 4 Thanon Kanphaengphet, Bangkok ⓣ (0) 2615 7333
ⓦ www.bkkchildrenmuseum.com ⓛ 09.00–17.00 Tues–Fri, 10.00–18.00 Sat & Sun ⓝ BTS Skytrain stop: Mo Chit; MRTA subway stop: Chatuchak Park ⓘ Admission charge

● Children having fun at the beach

Technopolis (National) Science Museum

Even children who hate science will adore this interactive museum that features English-speaking guides. Six floors of fun will keep them occupied and educated for at least half a day.

ⓐ Technopolis, Klong 5, Klong Luang, Pathum Thani ⓣ (0) 2577 9999 ext. 1850 ⓦ www.nsm.or.th ⓛ 09.30–17.00 Tues–Sun Ⓝ BTS Skytrain stop: Mo Chit; MRTA subway stop: Chatuchak Park. From either, take the red shuttle bus to Technopolis Park ❶ Admission charge

PONY & ELEPHANT RIDES

Hua Hin beach

A number of touts offer pony rides along Hua Hin beach. Prices are competitive, at about 600 baht per hour. As there are so many guides available, ask around for prices before agreeing to any journey. Always check the condition of the animal before starting out.

Pattaya Elephant Village

Elephant rides and shows are on offer, to the delight of young and old alike. Daily shows start at 14.30. Half-hour jungle treks on elephant back are also available.

ⓐ Reach via Siam Country Club Road east from Thanon Sukhumvit ⓣ (0) 3824 9818 ⓦ www.elephant-village-pattaya.com ❶ Admission charge

WATERSPORTS & SWIMMING

Many adventure operators offer snorkelling trips that allow older children to join in. Always check credentials before booking. When choosing a beach, ask around about undertow and wave conditions, as most Thai beaches do not have lifeguards. Keep watch over your kids at all times when using public and private facilities.

Sports & activities

GOLF

Thais are keen golfers, having learned the game from visiting Japanese and Koreans who love nothing more than to play a round or two during their holidays. Hua Hin is Thailand's principal golf destination. Bangkok and Pattaya also boast many courses to enjoy, some of championship quality, and Phuket has courses to cater to its large tourist population. Green fees are a lot less than you would pay at home. Book ahead if you want to play, especially during the high season, as waiting times can be long. Full listings of golf courses near you can be obtained from your hotel or visit ⓦ www.tourismthailand.org

HORSE RIDING

Enjoy a spot of horse riding either in the city or on the beach. Horses and ponies can be rented on the beaches of Hua Hin and Pattaya. For a ride in

⬥ *Well protected from the sun on Hua Hin golf course*

Bangkok, head over to the Garden City Polo Club to enjoy top-notch facilities, including jumping, dressage and individual coaching.

Garden City Polo Club ➌ Bangna-Trad Km 29, Rattanakosin 200 Pee Road, Bangbor, Samutprakarn ☎ (0) 2707 1534 Ⓦ http://gcpclub.tripod.com ⏰ 09.00–11.00, 14.30–16.30 Tues–Sun

MUAY THAI (KICKBOXING)

Muay thai is a form of kickboxing indigenous to Thailand. Now governed by the WBC (World Boxing Council), it is an internationally respected and practised combat form that combines elements of Buddhist religion, traditional dance and ritual in every bout. Each fight is accompanied by live drumming that gets faster as the bout progresses, in order to pick up the pace of the action. The sport is popular, so stadiums with regular matches are located across the country. The biggest matches are always held at Lumphini Stadium in Bangkok. If you want to try *muay thai* while you are in Thailand, enquire at the local stadium and you will be directed to a respected school. Be prepared to work out, though, as teachers don't go easy on you just because you're a foreigner.

❶ Information about matches at Lumphini and other major stadiums in Bangkok can be found at Ⓦ www.muaythaionline.org/features/thaistadiums.html

WATERSPORTS & DIVING

Diving, snorkelling, jet-skiing, yachting... it's all available in Thailand. If you can do it on, in or under water, you'll find someone here who has the equipment to facilitate you. Some of the best reefs for diving can be found in the waters near Krabi.

In recent years Koh Tao, located to the north of Koh Samui and Koh Pangan, has emerged as Thailand's hands-down premier destination for diving and dive instruction. The schools and tour operators here are organised in a local association that works to maintain high standards of equipment, instruction and safety.

Festivals & events

Thais love a good party. Combine that with a national religion that involves lots of special days of worship, and you have a country that can offer a festival or event almost every week. For details on when and where, visit the Tourism Authority of Thailand website (ⓦ www.tourismthailand.org).

JANUARY
National Children's Day Many parks, zoos and amusements offer free or discounted admission for kids on this annual day. If in Bangkok, take the children to the Grand Palace, where extra rooms are opened for one day only.

JANUARY/FEBRUARY
Chinese New Year Every Thai city has a large Chinese population, and New Year festivities always bring them out to celebrate. The biggest bash can be found in Bangkok, where firecrackers pop and dragons dance all day.

FEBRUARY/MARCH
Makha Bucha This Buddhist high holiday commemorates Buddha's last sermon before he reached nirvana. Temples get packed on the day with devotees and tourists looking to catch a glimpse of the goings-on.

APRIL
Songkram (Thai New Year) The party of the year as the hot season gets into full swing. *Farang* (foreigners) are major targets during this period, when tradition has locals throwing water at anyone and everyone within range. Expect to get soaked.

JULY/AUGUST
Asanha Bucha All Thai men are expected to devote a period of their life to the monkhood – usually up to a year. Asanha Bucha is the day when

they enter service, with their heads shorn as a symbol of their commitment. Temple visitation reaches a peak at this time, as people honour Buddha's first sermon after enlightenment.

OCTOBER

Ok Phansa Celebrate the end of the steamy rainy season on this day, considered to be the Buddhist equivalent of Lent. Monks become more solemn as all hair on the eyebrows and scalps is shaved off – again.

NOVEMBER

Pride Festivals The city of Pattaya kicks off the gay pride season with its annual celebration of all things sequinned. Further events are held in Bangkok in December and Phuket in March/April.

▶ A tuk-tuk *on a Krabi street*

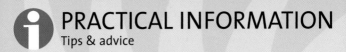

PRACTICAL INFORMATION
Tips & advice

Accommodation

Price ratings are based on a double room for one night.
£ = up to 1,000 baht   **££** = 1,000–2,000 baht   **£££** over 2,000 baht

BANGKOK
Sawasdee Khaosan Inn £ If you're looking for inexpensive digs in Bangkok or Pattaya, the Sawasdee chain is to be recommended. You may find cheaper rooms, but you won't find anyone who takes service and value more seriously. ⓐ 30 Rambuttri Road, Phra Nakorn
ⓣ (0) 2256 0890 ⓦ www.sawasdee-hotels.com

Mandarin Hotel ££ An attractive hotel offering relative luxury at a good price, with an easy walk to the Si Lom area, Lumphini Park, and Skytrain and subway stops. ⓐ 622 Rama IV Road, Si Lom ⓣ (0) 2238 0230
ⓦ www.mandarin-bkk.com

HUA HIN & CHA AN
Methavalai Hotel ££ An international-standard hotel in the middle of more lacklustre offerings in central Cha Am. Piano bar in the lobby.
ⓐ 220 Thanon Ruamjit, Cha Am ⓣ (0) 3243 3250 ⓦ www.methavalai.com

Sofitel Centara Grand Resort £££ Built in the 1920s, and lovingly restored, this is simply a beautiful piece of period resort architecture and elegance. Visit the grounds and have a meal or beverage, even if you don't stay here. ⓐ 1 Thanon Damnoenkasem, Hua Hin ⓣ (0) 3251 2021
ⓦ www.centarahotelsresorts.com

KOH CHANG
Thor's Palace £ Not like all the rest, not even a little bit. Spectacular ocean views from your balcony in a lovely and quirky stone building, all under the care of Koh Chang's most colourful and flamboyant entrepreneur. ⓐ Hat Sai Khao ⓣ (0) 3055 1160

KOH SAMUI

Rajapruek Samui Resort ££ Located on the quieter western coast of Samui, well away from the rowdiness of Chaweng, this could be an attractive choice for enjoying a relaxing stay on Thailand's most famous resort island. ⓐ 95/5 Moo 2, Lipa Noi, Thong Yang Beach ⓣ (0) 7742 3181 ⓦ www.rajaprueksamuiresort.com

Nora Beach Resort & Spa £££ Just a few minutes from the airport and Chaweng nightlife, this new resort offers affordable luxury and spectacular views. Weddings are a speciality. ⓐ 222 Moo 2, Chaweng Beach, Bophut ⓣ (0) 7741 3990 ⓦ www.norabeachresort.com

KRABI

Ao Nang Princeville Resort ££ Comfort and style at Krabi's most famous beach. Room service and the trappings of luxury at a good price. ⓐ 164 Moo 2, Ao Nang Beach, Mueang Krabi ⓣ (0) 7563 7971 ⓦ www.aonangprinceville.com

PATTAYA

Mind Resort ££ Convenient for Walking Street and all of central Pattaya's attractions, this simple but charming inn is girdled by greenery and is an oasis of comfort. ⓐ 171/16 Moo 10, Soi 17, Pattaya 3rd Road ⓣ (0) 3871 3030 ⓦ www.mindresortpattaya.com

PHUKET

The Old Phuket Hotel ££ This establishment is anything but old, being an elegant luxury hotel on Karon Beach. ⓐ 192/36 Karon Road, Karon ⓣ (0) 7639 6353 ⓦ www.theoldphuket.com

TRANG

Libong Nature Beach Bungalow £ A nature lover's paradise, with excursions to pirate caves, dugong sightings, sea gypsy villages and so on. ⓐ Koh Libong (Libong Island) ⓣ (0) 8 1894 6936 ⓦ www.trangsea.com

Preparing to go

GETTING THERE

By air

The only major international gateway serving Bangkok is Suvarnabhumi International Airport. The airport opened in late 2006 following numerous delays. Initially, there were problems with some of the facilities and there was concern about the usability of the new airport. However, these issues have been resolved and Suvarnabhumi now serves millions of passengers each year without any trouble. Some connecting flights to destinations within Thailand, however, have moved to the older airport at Don Muang. If your plans involve connecting at Bangkok for another location in Thailand, be sure to confirm whether your next flight will leave from the same airport.

Suvarnabhumi Airport ❶ (0) 2132 1888 ⓦ www.bangkokairportonline.com
Don Muang International Airport ⓦ www.donmuangairportonline.com

International airports also exist at Koh Samui, Phuket, Chiang Mai and Krabi, connecting to regional Asian destinations. Extensive domestic service is available with **Bangkok Airways** (ⓦ www.bangkokair.com), **AirAsia** (ⓦ www.airasia.com) and **Nok Air** (ⓦ www.nokair.com), as well as **Thai Airways International** (ⓦ www.thaiair.com).

These airlines compete strongly for domestic business. When you're planning your trip, take the time to compare fares. You may find some real bargain specials. Be aware, however, that a current 'trick' is to list a very low fare in the initial quote, which then increases hugely with taxes and surcharges when you go to check it out. Usually, you have to go a few steps beyond the first quote to find out what your real cost will be.

The following airlines offer non-stop services from London:

British Airways ❶ 0844 493 0787 ⓦ www.ba.com
Emirates ❶ 0870 243 2222 ⓦ www.emirates.com
EVA Air ❶ 020 7380 8300 ⓦ www.evaair.com
Qantas ❶ 0845 7747 767 ⓦ www.qantas.co.uk
Thai Airways International ❶ 0870 606 0911 ⓦ www.thaiair.com

Many people are aware that air travel emits CO_2, which contributes to climate change. You may be interested in the possibility of lessening the environmental impact of your flight through the charity Climate Care, which offsets your CO_2 by funding environmental projects around the world. Visit ⓦ www.climatecare.org

By rail
The only rail services that enter Thailand from a foreign country are those from Malaysia. It's a great way to see southern Thailand on your way up to Bangkok, or to get up into the hill country of the north. **State Railway of Thailand** ⓣ (0) 2621 8701 ⓦ www.railway.co.th

By ship
Cruising Southeast Asia is becoming more popular nowadays. For 5-star service and international standards, look to the Italian-based cruise line **Costa Cruises** (ⓦ www.costacruises.co.uk). Most seasons see at least one ship permanently routed in the region.

◔ *Pretty Hua Hin railway station*

Package holidays

Package holiday companies are increasingly diversifying their product offerings, with more and more unique properties coming online every day. Cost savings can be obtained due to the buying power of the operator, and you get the increased security of knowing that you have the back-up of the operator's staff throughout your holiday.

TOURISM AUTHORITY

The Tourism Authority of Thailand (TAT) is a valuable resource for leaflets, maps and general information about the country. There are branches all over Thailand, including one at Bangkok's Suvarnabhumi International Airport on the arrivals level. The main branch in Bangkok can help you plan itineraries, and many staff speak fluent English. Note that they cannot recommend specific companies.

TAT Main Branch ⓐ TAT Building, 1600 Thanon Petchaburi Tud Mai, Bangkok ❶ (0) 2250 5500 ⓦ www.tourismthailand-org ❶ 08.30–16.30 Mon–Fri ⓥ BTS Skytrain stop: Ratchathewi

BEFORE YOU LEAVE

It is advised, but not necessary, to get vaccinations for hepatitis A and B, polio, rabies, typhoid and tuberculosis before arriving in Thailand. Malaria is a possibility, but almost unheard of if you stick to the cities.

TRAVEL INSURANCE

Travel insurance is recommended for all travellers to Thailand. Policies should cover lost luggage, cancelled tickets and medical expenses including potential evacuation costs.

Online comparison sites, such as ⓦ www.moneysupermarket.com, provide an excellent one-stop-shop service that compares quotes from hundreds of suppliers. Please note that, if you plan to dive or undertake adventurous sports of any kind, you will need to check the fine print to see if you are covered. Extra charges may apply.

The Burmese, Cambodian and Laotian borders are malarial regions and therefore call for extra caution.

ENTRY FORMALITIES

Visitors to Thailand who are citizens of the UK, Ireland, the United States, Canada, Australia or New Zealand are given permission to enter the country visa-free and stay for up to 30 days. Visa regulations may change without notice, so be sure to double-check with the Thai embassy before departing. Your passport must be valid for at least six months after your date of arrival in Thailand, and you must have proof of an onward ticket out of the country.

Customs

Most personal effects and the following items are duty-free: 200 cigarettes or 250 g (9 oz) of cigars or smoking tobacco, 1 litre of wines or spirits, and photographic equipment (consisting of one still, video or movie camera plus five rolls of still film or three rolls of 8-mm or 16-mm motion-picture film).

Be warned that Thailand has strict controls regarding narcotics, firearms and pornography. Don't even think of transporting any such items into or out of the country; consequences are severe.

MONEY

The currency in Thailand is the baht (฿). The baht is divided into 100 satang. Notes are in denominations of 1,000, 500, 100, 50 and 20 baht, while coins are in denominations of 10, 5 and 1 baht and 50 satang and 25 satang. Try to get rid of large-denomination notes or change them at your hotel as fast as possible, as merchants and taxi drivers generally don't have large amounts of change.

You can withdraw money using ATMs widely distributed across Thailand. It is a good idea to carry at least two working cards with you, in case of any problem. Credit cards are widely accepted, but may require a surcharge, usually 3 per cent of the purchase price. Always keep an eye on who is handling your cards in order to avoid cloning scams. If you are given copies of slips, be sure to tear them up as soon as you receive them, to prevent duplication.

Banks will always provide the best rates of exchange, but opening times can be restrictive. Bureaux de change are more convenient due to their long opening hours and plentiful locations, but commission rates are high. If possible, avoid changing your money through your hotel, as rates will be to their advantage and not yours.

CLIMATE

While it is enjoyable to visit Thailand year-round, you may want to avoid the hot season from mid-March to mid-May, when the temperature can rise as high as 40°C (104°F). While it is possible to have fun in the city during this time, the sweltering humidity will quickly sap you of your energy, confining most of your temple-hopping to the early morning or late afternoon when the sun isn't quite as baking.

The rainy season occurs from May to October. Downpours are mercifully brief but they are severe, and the regular drenchings can create havoc, making long-distance travel a bit of a nightmare. November through to February are the months to visit if you want sunny, warm, clear days and breezy nights. Unfortunately, everyone and their mother travels during this time, and your empty poolside paradise could become a mob scene.

BAGGAGE ALLOWANCE

Airline baggage allowances are changing all the time, with some carriers imposing limits of as little as 20 kg (44 lb) per bag per person. Your baggage allowance will be confirmed with you when you book your tickets or when they are issued by the airline.

During your stay

AIRPORTS

These airlines all offer extensive domestic service in Thailand.

AirAsia ☎ (0) 2515 9999 Ⓦ www.airasia.com

Bangkok Airways ☎ (0) 2265 5678 Ⓦ www.bangkokair.com

Nok Air ☎ (0) 2627 2000 Ⓦ www.nokair.com

Thai Airways International ☎ (0) 2288 7000 Ⓦ www.thaiair.com

For information regarding services and transport to and from local airports, contact the airport in question:

Chiang Mai International Airport ☎ (0) 5327 0222 Ⓦ www.airportthai.co.th

Don Muang International Airport ☎ (0) 2535 1111 Ⓦ www.donmuangairportonline.com

Hat Yai International Airport ☎ (0) 7425 1007 Ⓦ www.airportthai.co.th

Koh Samui International Airport Koh Samui Airport is owned and operated by Bangkok Airways, but Thai Airways also flies in and out of Samui. ☎ (0) 2265 5678 Ⓦ www.samuiairportonline.com

Krabi International Airport ☎ (0) 7563 6541 Ⓦ www.krabi-tourism.com

Phuket International Airport ☎ (0) 7632 7230 Ⓦ www.airportthai.co.th

Suvarnabhumi International Airport ☎ (0) 2132 1888 Ⓦ www.bangkokairportonline.com

U-Tapao (Pattaya) International Airport ☎ (0) 3824 5595 Ⓦ www.utapao.com

COMMUNICATIONS

Phones

Public phones accept coins or phonecards. Some payphones also accept credit cards for international calls. Local calls cost 1 baht for every three minutes. Area codes must always be used in Thailand.

Mobile phones

Mobile service is available throughout Thailand, but international calls can be expensive. Using your own phone in Thailand will be costly; prices vary according to your service plan and provider. If you intend to make a number of domestic calls during your stay, consider investing in a prepaid local phone, which should cost you about 3,500 baht. Prepaid cards can be purchased from phone shops and many convenience stores.

Postal services

Postal services are quick and efficient. Stamps can be bought at post offices or from most convenience stores. Sending postcards abroad costs 12–19 baht. The service is generally reliable. Post offices are easy to spot. Look for the symbol of an envelope in the shape of a paper aeroplane featuring the colours of the Thai flag – red, white and blue.

Internet access

Internet access is available almost everywhere, with cafés offering terminals all over the country. If you find yourself in Bangkok, the Khao San Road, due to its huge backpacker population, is a good place to head

TELEPHONING THAILAND
To dial Thailand from abroad, dial the international access code (00), the country code (66), then the area code minus the initial 0 (e.g. 2 for Bangkok).

TELEPHONING ABROAD
When making an international call from Thailand, dial 00 for an international connection, followed by your country code (UK 44, Republic of Ireland 353, USA and Canada 1, Australia 61, New Zealand 64, South Africa 27), then the area code (leaving out the first 0 if there is one) and the local number.

OPERATOR ASSISTANCE
English-speaking operators can be reached to assist with both domestic and international calls by dialling 100.

for cheap, reliable and fast service. Other resorts offer services in major shopping centres or at prominent hotel complexes.

CUSTOMS

In Thailand, there are many customs you should be aware of. Very importantly, you must remove your shoes before you enter a temple. Buddhists consider the foot an unclean part of the body, while the head is regarded as sacred. You should never show your foot or the sole of your shoe to a Thai person nor touch the top of their head. Patting a child's head is therefore an absolute no-no.

Women should avoid touching a monk at all costs. If you happen to touch one, he will be forced to undergo a cleansing ritual that makes your daily shower look inadequate. If you want to pass a monk something, either leave it on the ground in front of him or give it to a man to pass to him.

When greeting a Thai, the polite thing to do is to 'wai' – put the palms of your hands together in front of your face and bow. And finally, if anything goes wrong during your stay, it is best to stay calm. Thai people do not react well to screaming and shouting – and you will lose much face if you resort to anger.

DRESS CODES

Thais are very conservative when it comes to dress. When visiting a religious or royal site, women must wear long skirts or trousers, and cover their shoulders. Men must also wear long trousers and shirts. On beaches, topless or nude bathing is not permitted. Bikinis can be worn on the beach, but should be covered up everywhere else.

ELECTRICITY

The standard electrical supply is 220 V, so you will need a transformer if you're using 110-V appliances. Two-pin plugs are the norm; plug adaptors can be purchased at most electrical shops in Thailand if you forget to bring one with you. Blackouts are common in rural regions, so a torch or candles are a must when travelling in these areas. If you are plugging in valuable electronics, surge protectors are advised.

EMERGENCIES

EMERGENCY NUMBERS

24-hour emergency services (police, fire, ambulance) can be reached by dialling 191 or 123. However, staff manning these lines generally speak little or no English. If a Thai person is available to make the call, you'll do much better. The Thai Tourist Police maintain a 24-hour line at 1155 with English-speaking staff available, although it's often hard to get through to this number.

Medical emergencies

Pharmacies are located throughout Thailand and many are open 24 hours. Many drugs that are prescription-only in most other countries can be picked up off the shelves at Thai pharmacies.

While there are hospitals located throughout the country, the best are in Bangkok. In the event of a serious mishap, go straight to the hospital nearest you, or, better, try to get to Bangkok for a chance to see some of Thailand's top doctors. Regional hospitals may have challenges understanding you in English, so an interpreter may be required during your examination.

Thailand is famous for cheap dentistry – especially if you are looking for procedures such as laser whitening and cosmetic dentistry. Many visitors come just to get dentistry performed as part of their holiday. Clinics are located throughout the country, and quality is generally high. Prices are a lot less than you would have to pay at home.

Bangkok Hospital ⓐ 2 Soi Soonvijai 7, Bangkok ⓣ (0) 2310 3000
ⓦ www.bangkokhospital.com ⓝ BTS Skytrain stop: Thong Lo
Bumrungrad Hospital ⓐ 33 Sukhumvit Soi 3, Bangkok ⓣ (0) 2667 1000
ⓦ www.bumrungrad.com ⓝ BTS Skytrain stop: Ploenchit

Police

In the event that you require police assistance, your first contact should be the Tourist Police on 1155. A report will need to be filled out for insurance purposes if you are the victim of a crime or have experienced the loss of a valuable item. Make sure to get it signed, stamped and dated before walking away from the station.

Lost property

If you lose anything or suspect that it has been stolen, contact the police immediately. If you lose an item on public transport, lost property offices may be found at major train and bus stations. If you lose something on a flight, check with the airline desk of your carrier.

Consulates & embassies

Consulates and embassies can assist you in certain emergencies, but they cannot provide you with funds if you find yourself stranded. Most embassies have lists of English-speaking doctors, dentists and lawyers that you can access when required.

American Embassy ⓐ 120–122 Thanon Witthayu ⓣ (0) 2205 4000 ⓦ http://bangkok.usembassy.gov ⓒ 07.00–16.00 Mon–Fri

Australian Embassy ⓐ 37 Thanon Sathorn Tai ⓣ (0) 2344 6300 ⓦ www.austembassy.or.th ⓒ 08.00–17.00 Mon–Fri

British Embassy ⓐ 14 Thanon Witthayu ⓣ (0) 2305 8333 ⓦ http://ukinthailand.fco.gov.uk/en ⓒ 08.00–16.30 Mon–Thur, 08.00–13.00 Fri

Canadian Embassy ⓐ 15th Floor, Abdul Rahim Place, 990 Thanon Rama IV ⓣ (0) 2636 0540 ⓦ http://geo.international.gc.ca/asia/bangkok ⓒ 07.30–16.00 Mon–Thur, 07.30–13.00 Fri

Irish Embassy ⓐ Ireland House, The Amp Walk, 218 Jalan Ampang, Kuala Lumpur, Malaysia ⓣ +603 2161 2963 ⓦ www.embassyofireland.my ⓒ 08.30–12.30 Mon–Fri

New Zealand Embassy ⓐ M Thai Tower, 14th Floor, All Seasons Place, 87 Thanon Witthayu ⓣ (0) 2254 2530 ⓦ www.nzembassy.com ⓒ 07.30–16.00 Mon–Fri

South African Embassy ⓐ M Thai Tower, 12th Floor, All Seasons Place, 87 Thanon Witthayu ⓣ (0) 2659 2900 ⓦ www.saembbangkok.com ⓒ 08.30–16.30 Mon–Thur, 07.30–13.30 Fri

GETTING AROUND

Car and motorcycle hire

Driving in Thailand should be approached with care. Traffic is often chaotic and drivers can be reckless. Fortunately, road signs today are virtually all dual-language, so navigation is not that hard. Having your own vehicle will make it easy for you to visit national parks and other sites that are less served by standard tours. The process of renting a car is extremely simple; in fact, official documents such as International Driver's Licences are rarely looked at, but have it to hand anyway. Motorcycle rentals are readily available in most locations and are an inexpensive way to make yourself mobile for local sightseeing.

Bus

Long-distance buses connect Thailand with most of Southeast Asia – Burma being the major exception. This is the only way to enter from Cambodia or Laos if you don't fly. Coaches also travel to and from the Golden Triangle region in the north and down to the Malaysian peninsula and Singapore. Service levels vary incredibly depending on how much you pay. You could be given anything from a cramped, livestock-packed bus to an air-conditioned luxury liner.

Bangkok is the main transfer point for all services, but you may have to transfer between stations across the city depending on where you are travelling to and from; each station takes its name from the direction it serves.

Eastern Bus Terminal ⓐ 300 Thanon Sukhumvit Ⓜ BTS Skytrain stop: Ekamai
Northern & Northeastern Bus Terminal ⓐ 999 Thanon Kamphaengphet 2 Ⓜ BTS Skytrain stop: Mo Chit; MRTA subway stop: Chatuchak Park. Take Bus no 3 to the terminal
Southern Bus Terminal ⓐ 147 Thanon Boromratchachonnani
Ⓜ Not accessible easily by public transport. Taxi recommended

HEALTH, SAFETY & CRIME

Many foreign nationals arrive in Thailand every year to take advantage of the cheap, high-quality health services provided in the country. Be sure to do your research, as there are many fly-by-night operators. For serious emergencies, go directly to the emergency departments of the main public hospitals.

During the wet season, dengue fever becomes an issue, so try to avoid being bitten by mosquitoes by using a good-quality repellent at all times. Also, keep covered up at peak bite times during the day, wear bright clothing and stay away from sources of stagnant water. Please note that there is no known cure for dengue fever, so once you see signs of a rash you should report to a doctor immediately.

Tap water is not advised unless you are in a 5-star resort or international-quality hotel. Ask in advance if your place of residence has a filtration system. Avoid accepting ice in your drinks while on the street. When in doubt, purchase bottled water from the numerous street vendors. Try to avoid adding to the massive litter problem by recycling whenever possible.

Street food is one of the highlights of any visit to Thailand, but you should check dishes for quality before ingesting. If you see any sign of pinkness in poultry, do not eat it. If you are concerned in any way, stick to vegetarian dishes to stay safe.

Crimes against tourists are rare but do occur. Pickpocketing and gem scams are the two most frequent incidents. Male 'guides' may also hassle you around major sights.

MEDIA

According to the law, freedom of expression and access to information are rights protected by the constitution. This law is often broken, however, due to constant changes in the government and regular

SMOKING

Regulations imposed by the Thai government mean that smoking is prohibited inside any air-conditioned public buildings or methods of transport. Bars and clubs are usually exempt (or choose to ignore the rule). If you need a puff, you'll either have to go outside or find an establishment with an outdoor patio or deck.

reversions to dictatorial rule. News outlets – both print and broadcast – are often faced with strong-arm tactics to showcase government propaganda stories, and lurid headlines are the order of the day. While crimes against foreigners rarely occur, they always eat up the front pages whenever something untoward happens.

Print

The best resource for international news in English is the *Bangkok Post*. While it has a heavy Bangkok bias, it's a good resource for what's going on around the world. Fridays have listings detailing what's on in your neck of the woods.

More local and specialised publications include *BK* (a Bangkok-based version of *Time Out*) and *Untamed Travel* (news and reviews pertinent to backpackers). For a bit of glitz and glamour, pick up a copy of the *Thailand Tatler*.

Each resort community has an English-language publication of its own, but most are purely driven by advertising revenue and are extremely editorially biased.

Radio

Public and privately owned stations broadcast in both Thai and English, but Thai predominates in rural and remote locations. News bulletins can be heard on Radio Thailand. Most stations play a combination of Thai and Western pop music. If you're looking for a cultural experience, you may want to reconsider turning on the radio. Céline Dion ballads and synthetic romance are a common feature.

Television

There isn't much choice in terms of Thai television, unless you are a fan of colourful game shows, beauty pageants, soap operas and talk shows. A quick glance will make you feel as if you've watched endless hours of daytime TV. Two television stations (Channels 3 and 7) are privately owned and more commercial in output. Here is where you will find things such as the local version of *Big Brother*. The other stations are either government or army owned and heavily censored as a result. If given the chance, Thais will keep their televisions tuned on private stations whenever possible. The only exception is if there is an important function involving the beloved royal family, when the government-owned networks get all the good stuff.

Hotels and resorts often provide satellite feed, including stations such as CNN, BBC World, MTV Asia and Star World.

OPENING HOURS
These may vary, but generally adhere to the following times:

Banks 09.30–15.30 Mon–Fri

Cultural institutions 08.30–16.00 Wed–Sun (although extended hours sometimes occur when major exhibitions hit town)

Government and private sector offices 08.30–16.30 Mon–Fri

Nightclubs and bars 01.00 closing time (although underground venues do exist; make friends with locals to find out where they are)

Shopping centres 10.00–22.00

RELIGION
Buddhism
About 95 per cent of Thais follow Theravada Buddhism. This form of the religion puts the responsibility of worship and enlightenment in the hands of the individual rather than society in general. As such, practices can vary wildly according to the determination of the person in question to reach nirvana.

In order to reach spiritual enlightenment, Thais practise a number of daily rituals to better their karma. Common actions include the feeding of monks, temple donations and regular worship at their local *wat* (temple). On high holidays, almost every member of society heads to the temple in order to score a few bonus points.

Unlike in Western religions, there is no specific day of worship; rather, Thais visit the *wat* at all times of the week – on the way to or from work, on the anniversary of a loved one's death, on the birth of a relative, or just because they feel like it.

All male Thai Buddhists are expected to devote a period of their life to the monkhood. Most choose to do this upon completing their studies before marriage or the beginning of their career. Consequently, you will always see a number of fresh-faced monks in saffron robes all over the country. Women are advised not to go near them, as they cannot be touched by females during their period of study. If they do come into physical contact with the opposite sex, they are required to go through an extensive cleansing ritual. If you want to donate or offer something to a monk, place the item on the ground so that there is no chance for you to come into contact with him. Additionally, when riding on public transport, keep an eye out for sections reserved for monks in order to assist them with their need for seclusion.

🔺 *Monks asking for alms*

Islam

People of Muslim faith are found throughout Thailand, but are concentrated in the southern provinces. The three southernmost provinces (Pattani, Yala, Narathiwat) make up the once-independent region called Pattani, and today are the site of an ongoing violent rebellion. At this time, travel in this part of Thailand is strongly discouraged. In other parts of the country, relations between the faiths are good.

Western religions

Few locals practise Western religions such as Christianity or Judaism. However, there are places of worship established for expats and visitors, especially in Bangkok. If you are in search of a church or synagogue, ask your hotel reception for directions and information.

TIME DIFFERENCES

Clocks in Thailand are seven hours ahead of Greenwich Mean Time. In Bangkok at 12.00, times elsewhere are as follows:

Australia Eastern Standard Time 15.00, Central Standard Time 14.30, Western Standard Time 13.00
New Zealand 17.00
South Africa 07.00
UK and Republic of Ireland 05.00
US and Canada Newfoundland Time 01.30, Atlantic Canada Time 01.00, Eastern Standard Time 24.00 (same day), Central Time 23.00, Mountain Time 22.00, Pacific Time 21.00, Alaska 18.00 (previous day)

TIPPING

Tipping is common in Thailand, but not to the same degree as you would find in the West. Locals tend to tip poorly – 20 baht or so for a waiter, or 5 baht for a taxi journey. More common is the practice of tipping before a meal or hotel stay to ensure that you are well cared for throughout your visit. Most Thais in the service industry are paid shockingly low wages, so anything you provide is appreciated. Locations that add on service charges usually do not divide the monies among their staff, so try to shell out a little extra. Masseurs especially appreciate any extra you can give them, as most of the funds you pay at the end of the treatment go straight to the owner of the establishment.

If you are on a tour, guides, drivers and hotel maids are generally expected to receive something at the end for their trouble, even if it is just 20 baht.

TOILETS

Public toilets are few in Thailand, and the ones that do exist are positively foul. If you are caught short, head to the nearest shopping centre, department store or temple. You may have to spend a couple of baht for access. Always come prepared with toilet paper, as it may not be provided. Many public conveniences will be squat-style with a plastic dipper used for cleansing. If you need facilities badly and are close to a restaurant or bar, feel free to walk in to use the loo, but always ask management before doing so. In most cases you will be permitted with no questions asked.

TRAVELLERS WITH DISABILITIES

Facilities for visitors with disabilities are generally poor in Thailand. Pavements are cracked, and there aren't any bevelled kerbs to assist with access. Thai religious and cultural beliefs often mean that the nation's disabled citizens are kept at home. However, you will see many limbless beggars in the streets. Be warned that donations to them may not go into their pockets, as many of these unfortunate souls are actually enslaved by the local mafia and forced on the street to beg.

For advice or help in planning a stay, disabled visitors should try contacting the following:

Tourism Authority of Thailand ⓦ www.tourismthailand.org